OECD Urban Studies

The Circular Economy in Groningen, the Netherlands

This document, as well as any data and map included herein, are without prejudice to the status of or sovereignty over any territory, to the delimitation of international frontiers and boundaries and to the name of any territory, city or area.

Please cite this publication as:
OECD (2020), *The Circular Economy in Groningen, the Netherlands*, OECD Urban Studies, OECD Publishing, Paris, *https://doi.org/10.1787/e53348d4-en*.

ISBN 978-92-64-64972-9 (print)
ISBN 978-92-64-72442-6 (pdf)

OECD Urban Studies
ISSN 2707-3432 (print)
ISSN 2707-3440 (online)

Preface

We are very proud to introduce the results of an 18-month policy dialogue with 30+ stakeholders to shape a vision and strategy for a circular economy in the city of Groningen, Netherlands as part of the OECD Programme on the Circular Economy in Cities and Regions.

In the face of megatrends such as population growth in cities, urbanisation and climate change, the transition to a circular economy is becoming an imperative for cities of all sizes to reduce the pressure on natural resources, while addressing new infrastructure, services and housing needs, and boosting economic growth and environmental quality. Cities and regions are at the core of citizen well being, in areas such as transport, solid waste, water or energy.

Moving from a "take-make-dispose" linear system to one in which resource waste is prevented, implies going beyond solely technical aspects and ensure governance and economic conditions are met. For the circular economy to materialise, policies need to be aligned, stakeholders engaged, and legal and regulatory frameworks enabling innovation.

This report summarises important milestones achieved so far. Its analytical framework puts People, Firms and Places at the centre of the shift towards a circular economy. It puts forward bold recommendations and concrete actions for Groningen to act as promoter, facilitator and enabler of this transition. This requires political leadership and commitment towards the transition to sustainable pathways, as well as multi-stakeholder and multi-sectoral approaches, and new business models.

An important part of the work was the bottom-up and inclusive policy dialogue, whereby each stakeholder could share experience, listen and learn from each other, and benefit from expertise and guidance from peer cities and the OECD team.

While we are aware that we are just at the beginning of the transition from a linear to a circular economy in Groningen, the city is committed to implement these recommendations and raise their profile within our community and globally. The OECD Centre for Entrepreneurship, SMEs, Regions and Cities stands ready to support Groningen with this endeavour. This will be all the more relevant in the aftermath of the COVID-19 crisis, when cities and regions will be urged to reconsider the link between environment and health, reflect on the de-materialisation of the economy and society and on circular resources loops in response to the hyper-globalisation of the recent years. The OECD Programme on the Circular Economy in Cities and Regions will seek further opportunities, evidence and recommendations to make the circular economy part of the solution towards healthier, less resource wasteful and environmental aware societies.

Lamia Kamal-Chaoui	Glimina Chakor
Director, OECD Centre for Entrepreneurship, SMEs, Regions and Cities	Deputy Mayor of Groningen

Foreword

The circular economy is about preventing wasted resources through reusing materials, improving design to increase the durability of goods and products, and transforming waste.

Population growth, climate change and urbanisation are likely to increase the pressure on natural resources, as well as the demand for new infrastructure, services and housing. By 2050, the global population will reach 9 billion people, 70% of which will be living in cities. Cities represent almost two-thirds of global energy demand, produce up to 80% of greenhouse gas emissions and 50% of global waste.

Cities and regions play a fundamental role in shifting from a linear to a circular economy, as they are responsible for key decisions in local public services such as transport, solid waste, water and energy that affect citizens' well-being, economic growth and environmental quality. In cities and regions, the circular economy should ensure that:

- *services* (e.g. from water to waste and energy) are provided while preventing waste generation, making efficient use of natural resources as primary materials, optimising their reuse and allowing synergies across sectors;
- *economic activities* are planned and executed in a way to close, slow and narrow loops across value chains, and
- *infrastructure* is designed and built to avoid linear locks-in, which use resources intensively and inefficiently.

The OECD Programme on the Circular Economy in Cities and Regions was designed to support national and subnational governments in their transition towards the circular economy through evidence-based analysis, multi-stakeholder dialogues, tailored recommendations and customised action plans. The Programme relies on a consortium of cities and countries engaged in peer-to-peer dialogues and knowledge sharing activities, including Glasgow (United Kingdom), Granada (Spain), Groningen (Netherlands), Umeå (Sweden), Valladolid (Spain) and Ireland.

This report summarises the findings from an 18-month policy dialogue with the city of Groningen, Netherlands to develop a vision for the circular economy transition and learn from existing best practices. In 2018, the municipal council of Groningen took the unanimous decision of making the circular economy a priority for the city, identifying three strategic areas: public procurement, waste and knowledge. Moreover, the circular economy is expected to contribute to two long-term objectives set by the municipality: to become CO_2 neutral by 2035 and to separate and reuse all waste by 2030. Last but not least, the city aims to foster the necessary conditions to create 5,000 new jobs by connecting the health, ICTs, energy, digital and creative industries to the circular economy.

Achieving these objectives entails providing space for experimentation, sharing knowledge, leading the co-ordination among stakeholders and defining a circular economy framework. This report also argues that a circular economy strategy in Groningen could build on the collaboration with the business, academic and non-for-profit sectors, and lead to the creation of a circular economy "ecosystem", through which fostering experimentation and innovation.

Acknowledgements

This report was prepared by the OECD Centre for Entrepreneurship, SMEs, Regions and Cities (CFE) led by Lamia Kamal-Chaoui, Director, as part of the Programme of Work and Budget of the Regional Development Policy Committee. It is the result of an 18-month policy dialogue with 30+ stakeholders from public, private, non-profit sectors and representatives from the municipality of Groningen, Netherlands.

The report and underlying policy dialogues were co-ordinated by Oriana Romano, Head of the Water Governance and Circular Economy Unit, under the supervision of Aziza Akhmouch, Head of the Cities, Urban Policies and Sustainable Development Division in the CFE. The report was drafted by a core OECD team of experts comprised of Oriana Romano, Luis Cecchi, Policy Analyst and Ander Eizaguirre, Junior Policy Analyst. Special thanks are conveyed to Marco Bianchini, Policy Analyst in the SME and Entrepreneurship Division in CFE, for his participation in the fact-finding mission, inputs and comments on earlier drafts.

The OECD Secretariat is grateful to the deputy Mayor of Groningen, Ms Glimina Chakor, for her high level of commitment and leadership towards circular economy in the city. Warm thanks are also extended to the admirable local team in Groningen led by Aline Otten, Economic Affairs Manager, for the excellent collaboration throughout the dialogue, in particular: Floor de Jong, Co-ordinator of International Affairs, and Anne Helbig, Policy Advisor.

Furthermore, the policy dialogue benefited from insights from peer reviewers who are warmly thanked for sharing their valuable expertise and city experience, participating in the case study missions and providing international best practices as well as guidance on the report, namely: Sebastian Holmström, Project Co-ordinator in the Communications and Spatial Planning Department (City of Umeå, Sweden); and Rosa Huertas Gonzalez, Director of the Innovation, Economic Development, Employment and Commerce Department (City of Valladolid, Spain). Special thanks are conveyed to Professor Jan Jonker, Chair of Sustainable Entrepreneurship, Nijmegen School of Management at Radboud University Nijmegen, Netherlands, for his contribution to the policy seminar, held on 17 September 2019 in Groningen, Netherlands.

This report is the result of the interviews with 30+ stakeholders during the OECD visits to Groningen, Netherlands (12-15 February and 17 September 2019) (Annex A), as well as insights from the OECD Survey on the Circular Economy in Cities and Regions and desk research. Interim findings and progress results were presented at the "Workshop: Circular Economy in Cities" during the 40th meeting of the Regional Development Policy Committee (5 November 2018, Paris, France), and at the 1st OECD Roundtable on the Circular Economy in Cities and Regions (4 July 2019, Paris, France).

The draft report benefited from written comments by stakeholders engaged throughout the policy dialogue, in particular: Eileen Blackmore (House of Design), Pieter Jan Bouwmeister (Province of Groningen), Cor Dijkstra (Kaaskop), Michael Freerks (Royal Haskoning DHV Nederland B.V.), Marco Kwak (Attero), Tjitse Mollema (Waterschap Noorderzijlvest), Mathijs Niehaus (DaaromWel), Elze Reitsema (van Wijnen) and Maarten Wiersma (ABC2).

The report was submitted to RDPC delegates for approval by written procedure by 6 March 2020 under the cote [CFE/RDPC/URB(2020)/5]. The final version was edited and formatted by Eleonore Morena, and François Iglesias and Pilar Philip prepared the manuscript for publication.

Table of contents

Tables

Figures

Boxes

Follow OECD Publications on:

http://twitter.com/OECD_Pubs

http://www.facebook.com/OECDPublications

http://www.linkedin.com/groups/OECD-Publications-4645871

http://www.youtube.com/oecdilibrary

http://www.oecd.org/oecddirect/

Abbreviations and acronyms

ACEF	Amsterdam Climate and Energy Fund
AMB	Barcelona Metropolitan Area (*Área Metropolitana de Barcelona*)
CBS	Statistics Netherlands
CFE	Centre for Entrepreneurship, SMEs, Regions and Cities
CISE	Cantabria Entrepreneurship Centre
CO_2	Carbon dioxide
EBG	Economic Board Groningen
EU	European Union
EUR	Euro
FEMP	Spanish Federation of Municipalities and Provinces (*Federación Española de Municipios y Provincias*)
GBP	British Pound
GDP	Gross domestic product
GHG	Greenhouse gas
ICT	Information and communications technology
Kwh	Kilowatt-hour
LCA	Life Cycle Assessment
LWARB	London Waste and Recycling Board
MW	Megawatt
NGO	Non-governmental organisation
NICE	Northern Innovation Circular Economy
NIMBY	Not In My Backyard
OECD	Organisation for Economic Co-operation and Development
PM_{10}	Particulate matter smaller than 10 microns in diameter
PRAE	Centre of Environmental Resources (*Centro de Recursos Ambientales*)
R&D	Research and development
RISN	Resource Innovation and Solutions Network
SDGs	Sustainable Development Goals
SME	Small- and medium-sized enterprise
SNN	Northern Netherlands Alliance (*Samenwerkingsverband Noord-Nederland*)
TJ	Terajoule
TNO	Netherlands Organisation for Applied Scientific Research (*Nederlandse Organisatie voor toegepastnatuurwetenschappelijk Onderzoek*)
UWV	Employee Insurance Schemes Implementing Body (*Uitvoeringsinstituut Werknemersverzekeringen*)

Executive summary

The city of Groningen, Netherlands, has been historically known for being located in a natural gas production area, which has been the country major supplier for the last 60 years. Following the decision of the Dutch National Cabinet to phase out gas production by 2022, the city set up the goal of becoming energy and CO2 neutral by 2035 and waste neutral by 2030. As such, Groningen is on the verge of a radical makeover and the circular economy is part of it.

Socioeconomic and environmental trends represent key drivers for the transition to a circular economy to take place: population growth, expected to reach almost 250 000 by 2038, generates the need for new houses (20 000 by 2030) that can be potentially built according to circular principles. New jobs opportunities are expected to develop at the crossroads of strategic sectors such as health, ITC, energy and creative industries to the circular economy, potentially reaching 5 000 new jobs in the short term.

In 2018, the City Council instructed the City Board to develop a sustainable and circular vision for the city and identified three strategic areas: i) public procurement, to foster the circular transition in the business sector; ii) waste management, setting the objective of becoming a waste neutral city by 2030; and, iii) knowledge, to create platforms to connect academia, businesses and civil society organisations with the municipality. A vice mayor with specific responsibilities regarding the circular economy also took office.

The circular transition is taking place step by step. Following the council's decision, the municipality initiated capacity-building programmes on Green Public Procurement (GPP) and opened a tender for a 10-year service of refurbished furniture. Moreover, the municipality committed to include circular criteria for waste processing in the new waste management concession after 2022. A Circular Economy Hub is planned as an incubator space for small businesses and start-ups, and as an information centre, repair hub and second-hand shop. In 2019, the city initiated the "Front-runner Project" to support small and medium-sized enterprises (SMEs) in the implementation of more sustainable and circular business models.

There are relevant strengths on which Groningen is building its own circular economy strategy: a vibrant start-up and business scene in the health, information and communications technology (ITC), energy, agro-food, chemical and creative sectors, counting on 20 000 companies; a strong academic community developing and testing solutions to increase resource efficiency in production systems, use alternative energy sources for transport or bio-based product from organic waste as raw material; and environmentally aware citizens.

Going forward, a full-fledge transition towards the circular economy will require overcoming a number of challenges:

- **Building a coherent narrative on the circular economy** across the wealth of existing sustainable initiatives with the aim of achieving common socioeconomic and environmental objectives;

- **Enhancing co-ordination** amongst provinces and with the region, also engaged in the transition to a circular economy;

- **Improving more systematic data collection** that could allow taking informed decisions, measuring progress and improving implementation;

- **Matching financial and human resources** to the actions required to move from a linear to a circular economy;
- **Further engaging with stakeholders**, contributing to create a circular economy culture.

The report recommends concrete actions to improve Groningen's ability to promote, facilitate and enable the circular economy. In particular:

- **To promote the circular economy**, the municipality could:
  - become a role model for business and citizens in embracing circular economy principles in daily activities;
  - develop a strategy on the circular economy to enhance coherence across existing initiatives and building a strong and global vision for the circular economy;
  - promote a circular economy culture and awards and certifications for circular economy projects, and;
  - support SMEs, entrepreneurs and start-ups by being the first customer of innovative products and goods.
- **To facilitate collaboration among a wide range of actors** to make the circular economy happen on the ground, the municipality could:
  - enhance co-ordination across municipal departments and across regional and provincial governments;
  - foster practice exchange amongst public, not-for-profit actors and businesses;
  - connect businesses and universities to stimulate innovation
  - strengthen existing networks to pick the "low-hanging fruits" from co-operation of local businesses;
  - establish a single-window for circular businesses and supporting entrepreneurship, and;
  - foster new cross-cutting solutions across urban and rural areas.
- **To enable the necessary governance and economic conditions**, the municipality could:
  - identify gaps and ways forward on how to adapt laws and regulations and financial and economic conditions for the implementation of circular economy initiatives;
  - implement green public procurement;
  - develop training programmes and build technical capacities;
  - create spaces for experimentation, and;
  - develop an information, monitoring and evaluation system.

1 Towards a circular economy in Groningen, Netherlands

This chapter provides an overview of the circular economy in cities and focuses on the rationale for the circular economy transition in the city of Groningen, Netherlands, by looking at main drivers leading to a shift from a linear to a circular economy, and socioeconomic and environmental data and trends.

Introduction: The circular economy in cities and regions

The transition to a circular economy is underway and cities and regions are at the centre of it. By 2050, the global population will reach 9 billion people, 70% of which will be living in cities (UN, 2018[1]). The pressure on natural resources will increase, while new infrastructure, services and housing will be needed. Already, cities represent almost two-thirds of global energy demand (IEA, 2016[2]) and produce up to 80% of greenhouse gas emissions (World Bank, 2010[3]). By 2050, urban dwellers will still be the most exposed to high concentrations of air pollutants[1] (OCDE, 2012[4]). Cities produce 50% of global waste (UNEP, 2013[5]). It is estimated that globally, by 2050, the levels of municipal solid waste will double (IEA, 2016[2]; UNEP/IWSA, 2015[6]). A total of 80% of food is consumed in cities and compared to today's levels, 60% more food will be required to feed the population in the coming decades (Ellen MacArthur Foundation, 2019[7]). At the same time, water stress and water consumption will increase by 55% by 2050 (OCDE, 2012[4]). Cities and regions have core responsibilities for local public services such as transport, solid waste, water and energy. As such, they are at the centre of key decisions having a strong impact on citizens' well-being, environmental quality and economic growth.

There is no unique definition for circular economy, which is now facing a validity challenge period. Although there are many definitions of the circular economy, they all include as a basic assumption the recognition of waste as a resource (Box 1.1). The circular economy is about preventing wasted resources through reusing materials, improving design to increase the durability of goods and products, and transforming waste. In cities and regions, the circular economy should ensure that: services (e.g. from water to waste and energy) are provided whilst preventing waste generation, making efficient use of natural resources as primary materials, optimising their reuse and allowing synergies across sectors; *economic activities* are planned and carried out in a way to close, slow and narrow loops across value chains and *infrastructure* is designed and built to avoid linear locks-in, which use resources intensively and inefficiently.

The circular economy is not an end per se, but a means to an end: it provides an opportunity to do more with less, to better use available natural resources, and to transform waste into new resources, while promoting new jobs opportunities and tackling inequalities (e.g. access to sharing services and commodities, form mobility to agro-food, to buildings). As such, while the environmental narrative, whereby less use of materials implies reduced greenhouse gas (GHG) emissions, has been so far predominant in promoting the shift to a circular economy, cities and regions are increasingly paying attention to the social and economic aspects as drivers for this transition. According to Blomsma and Brennan (2017[8]), the circular economy is now facing its "validity challenge period" on its way to becoming a robust and consolidated concept, implying a radical shift in consumer behaviour.

Box 1.1. Examples of circular economy definitions

- "The circular economy is where the value of products, materials and resources is maintained in the economy for as long as possible, and the generation of waste minimised." (EC, 2015[9])

- "The circular economy is restorative and regenerative by design. Relying on system-wide innovation, it aims to redefine products and services to design waste out while minimising negative impacts. A circular economy is then an alternative to a traditional linear economy (make, use, dispose)." (Ellen MacArthur Foundation, 2018[10])

- "An economic system that replaces the end-of-life concept, with reducing, alternatively using, recycling and recovering materials in production/distribution and consumption processes. It operates at the micro level (products companies, consumers), the meso level (eco-industrial parks) and the macro level (city, region, nation and beyond), with the aim of accomplishing sustainable development, thus simultaneously creating environmental quality, economic

---

- prosperity and social equity, to the benefit of current and future generations. It is enabled by novel business models and responsible consumers." (Kirchherr, Reike and Hekkert, 2017[11])

- "The circular economy is one that has low environmental impacts and that makes good use of natural resources, through high resource efficiency and waste prevention, especially in the manufacturing sector, and minimal end-of-life disposal of materials." Ekins et al. (2019[12]).

- "There are three different layers of circularity, with increasingly broad coverage: i) closing resource loops; ii) slowing resource loops; and iii) narrowing resource loops. All these explicitly or implicitly aim at addressing the market failures associated with materials use, the failure to address local environmental consequences associated with extraction; or the failure to include the environmental externalities associated with waste generation". Furthermore, there are economic inefficiencies associated with the inefficient use of scarce resources." (OECD, 2019[13])

Source: EC (2015[9]), *Closing the Loop – An EU Action Plan for the Circular Economy*, European Commission, https://eur-lex.europa.eu/legal-content/EN/TXT/HTML/?uri=CELEX:52015DC0614&from=EN (accessed on 21 February 2020); Ellen McArthur Foundation (2018[10]), *What is a Circular Economy?*, https://www.ellenmacarthurfoundation.org/circular-economy/concept (accessed on 21 February 2020); Kirchherr, J., D. Reike and M. Hekkert (2017[11]), *Conceptualizing the Circular Economy: An Analysis of 114 Definitions*, http://dx.doi.org/10.1016/j.resconrec.2017.09.005; Ekins et al. (2019[12]), "The Circular Economy: What, Why, How and Where", Background paper for an OECD/EC Workshop on 5 July 2019 within the workshop series "Managing environmental and energy transitions for regions and cities", Paris; OECD (2019[13]), *Global Material Resources Outlook to 2060: Economic Drivers and Environmental Consequences*, https://doi.org/10.1787/9789264307452-en.

The circular economy in cities and regions is expected to generate a positive impact on economic growth, the creation of new jobs and the reduction of negative impacts on the environment. By 2030, shifting from a linear approach of "take, make and dispose" to a circular system is estimated to hold a potential of USD 4.5 trillion for economic growth (Accenture, 2015[14]). Projections show that, by 2030, resource productivity in Europe can improve by 3% and generate a gross domestic product (GDP) increase of up to 7% (McKinsey Centre for Business and Environment, 2016[15]). Projections at the city level show that for example, applying a circular economy approach to the construction chain in the city of Amsterdam (Netherlands) would decrease GHG emissions by half a million tonnes of CO_2 per year. In London (United Kingdom), the benefits from circular approaches applied to the built environment, food, textiles, electricals and plastics are estimated at GBP 7 billion every year by 2036.[2] About 50 000 jobs related to the circular economy are estimated to be created in the Île-de-France region.[3] Environmental benefits consist of: decreased pollution; increased share of renewable or recyclable resources; and reduced consumption of raw materials, water, land and energy (EEA, 2016[16]). Yet, the transition should be "just" by taking into account people' social well-being, quality of life and equity.

The potential of the circular economy still needs to be unlocked. Today, less than 10% of the global economy is circular (Circle Economy, 2020[17]). Unlocking the potential of the circular economy in cities and regions implies going beyond solely technical aspects and putting the necessary governance in place to create incentives (legal, financial), stimulate innovation (social, institutional) and generate information (data, knowledge, capacities). It would also mean looking at the barriers for businesses to "close the loops", by re-thinking business models (e.g. leasing and sharing) and analysing the economic instruments that could support the transition in several sectors, including waste, food, built-up environments and water. The circular economy implies governance models based on multi-stakeholder and multi-sectoral approaches. For the circular economy to happen, policies need to be aligned, stakeholders informed and engaged, legal and regulatory frameworks updated and in support of innovation.

The drivers for the circular transition in Groningen, Netherlands

The circular economy in Groningen, as an opportunity for innovation and sustainable waste management, is a policy priority. According to the OECD Survey on the Circular Economy in Cities and Regions (OECD, 2019[18]), the words that the city associated the most with the circular economy are "raw material", "zero waste" and "innovation" (the bigger the word in the figure, the higher the importance) (Figure 1.1). This reflects the intention of the city to combine innovation (e.g. in design and planning) with a more sustainable waste management approach that is able to minimise waste production and transform waste into resources (OECD, 2019[18]). This echoes the municipal council's political commitment: in June 2018, it took the unanimous decision of making the circular economy a priority for the city (Chapter 2). The transition from a linear to a circular economy entails providing space for experimentation, sharing knowledge, leading the co-ordination among stakeholders and defining a circular economy framework (Groningen Municipality, 2018[19]). Importantly, a vice-mayor with responsibilities regarding the circular economy took office after the elections in November 2018 (Box 1.2).

Figure 1.1. Tag cloud on the circular economy in Groningen, Netherlands

Note: The respondent had to choose the top 5 words most often associated with the circular economy. The answer is based on the following question: "Please indicate the top 5 words from the list suggested below you most often associate with the circular economy in your context, ranking from 1 (most important) to 5 (less important)".
Source: Own elaboration based on the city of Groningen's answers to the OECD (2019[18]) OECD Survey on the Circular Economy in Cities and Regions.

Box 1.2. The institutional organisation of local governments in the Netherlands

The municipal council

The municipal council is an elected body with administrative, legislative and budgetary powers. The size of the municipal council depends on the size of the municipality: from 9 (municipalities with less than 3 000 inhabitants) to 45 seats (municipalities with over 200 000 inhabitants). Municipal council representatives are elected every four years. The municipal council oversees the municipal executive by critically assessing its performance. It is responsible for controlling the mayor and the vice-mayors. The mayor chairs the council but has no right to vote; vice-mayors are not allowed to be members of the municipal council. Full council meetings and committee meetings are open to the public. In order to encourage participation in local politics, municipalities offer citizens the opportunity to intervene in committee meetings and sometimes also during plenary sessions.

Figure 1.2. Institutional map of Groningen municipality, Netherlands

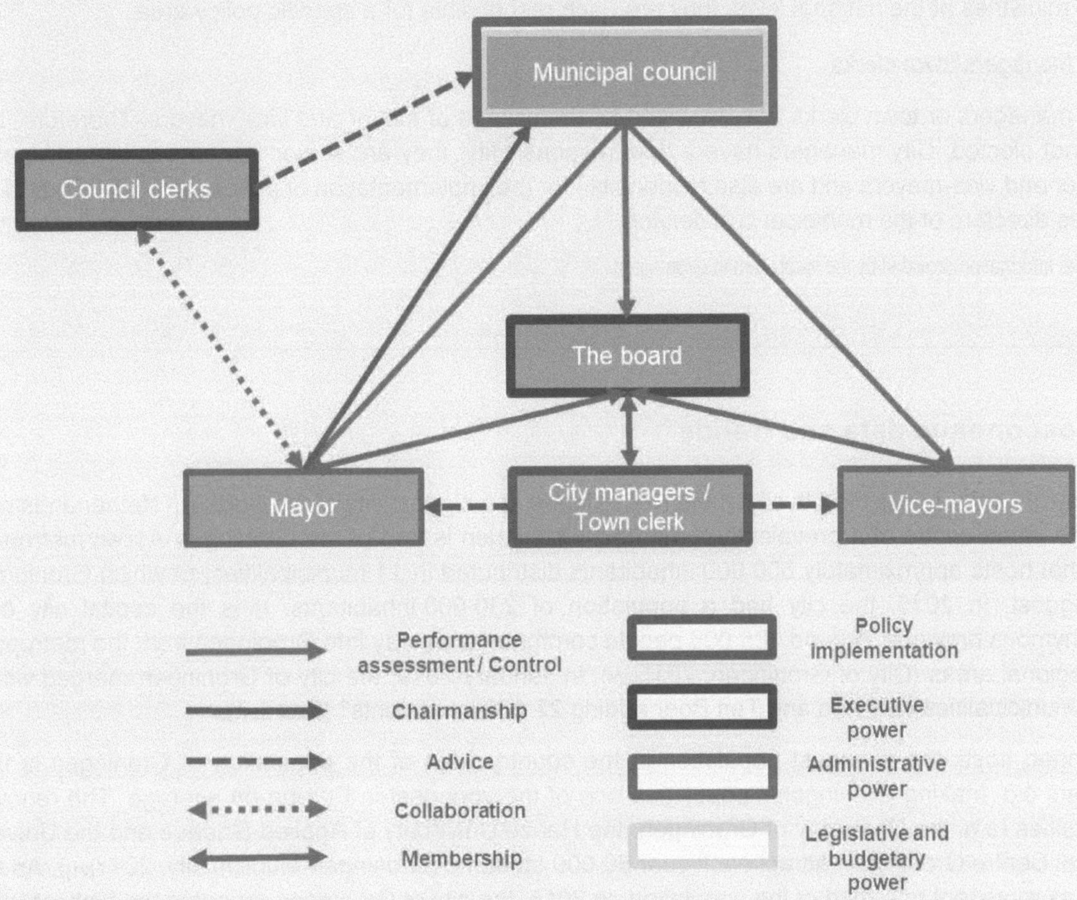

Council clerks

Council clerks are the most important advisors to municipal councils and play a vital and supporting role for council members, political parties and council committees. They are appointed and dismissed, if necessary, by a vote of the municipal council. They work alongside members of the executive, in particular, the mayor.

The executive (or board): Colleges of mayors and vice-mayors

Executive power is wielded by colleges of mayor and vice-mayors. The colleges are responsible for governing municipalities and leading the public administration. They are accountable to the council. The internal distribution of tasks differs according to the local circumstances in each municipality.

Mayors

Mayors chair municipal councils and executive colleges. They act as intermediaries between the parties and ensure continuity. Therefore, they do not usually propose regulations or policies. The mayoral term lasts six years. This term may be renewed on the recommendation of the municipal council. Mayors can be reappointed, although it is rare for mayors to serve for more than two terms and exceptional to serve for more than three.

Vice-mayors

Along with mayors, vice-mayors are the other administrators of local government. The number of vice-mayors depends on the size of the municipality (from 2 to 9). In Groningen, there are seven vice-mayors. Like ministries at the national level, they are each responsible for a specific policy area.

City managers/town clerks

City managers or town clerks are employed by the college of mayor and vice-mayors. Therefore, they are not elected. City managers have a dual responsibility: they are senior advisors to the colleges of mayor and vice-mayors and are also responsible for the implementation of policies and decisions. They act as directors of the municipal civil service.

Source: Information provided by the local team in Groningen.

Socioeconomic data and trends

The city of Groningen is the 6th city of the Netherlands, the biggest city of the Northern Netherlands region and the urban centre of a prevalently rural area. Groningen is part of the Groningen-Assen metropolitan area that hosts approximately 500 000 inhabitants distributed in 11 municipalities, of which Groningen is the biggest. In 2015, the city had a population of 230 000 inhabitants. It is the capital city of the homonymous province. Around 185 000 people commute every day into Groningen from the metropolitan and regional areas (City of Groningen, 2015[20]). In January 2019, the city of Groningen merged with the small municipalities of Haren and Ten Boer adding 27 000 inhabitants[4] (Box 1.3).

Groningen hosts the youngest population in the country. Half of the population of Groningen is under 35 years old, making Groningen's population one of the youngest in Europe on average. The renowned universities (e.g. the University of Groningen, the Hanze University of Applied Science and the University Medical Centre Groningen) attract each year 60 000 students (Groningen Municipality, 2017[21]). As such, students represent one-third of the population. In 2015, the city of Groningen recorded the highest level of satisfaction regarding the provision of education and training in the European Union (EU) (Eurostat, 2019[22]).

Box 1.3. Demographic, administrative and economic structure of the Northern Netherlands region

The Netherlands is composed of 4 regions and 12 provinces. Groningen is located in the Northern Netherlands region, which includes the provinces of Drenthe, Friesland and Groningen (Figure 1.3). Groningen is the largest city and the biggest functional urban area[5] in the region, which hosts 775 000 inhabitants. The Northern Netherlands region is defined as a "frontier region"[6] alongside the North Holland region, which includes Amsterdam, and the South Holland region, that includes Rotterdam and The Hague. The region's industrial cluster, formed by 31 companies and organisations in the provinces of Drenthe and Groningen, has set the goal to become Europe's most sustainable industrial area by 2030 (Groningen Seaports, 2018[23]).

Figure 1.3. Map of Groningen, Netherlands

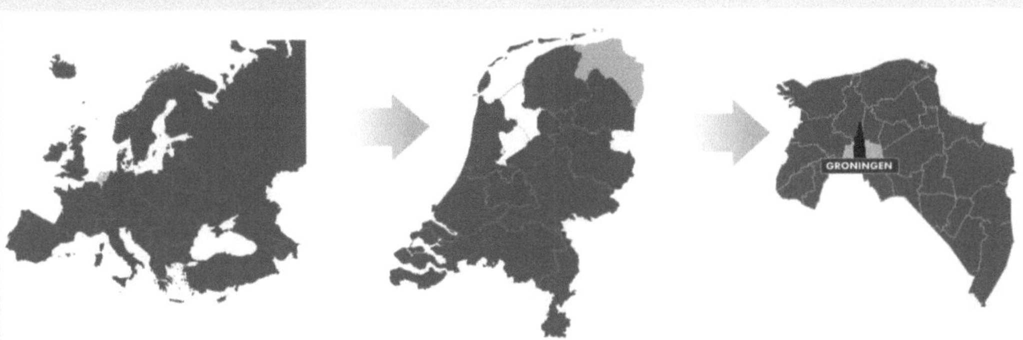

Source: Groningen Municipality (2018[24]), *Demografische ontwikkelingen gemeente Groningen*, http://www.oisgroningen.nl (accessed on 30 April 2019).

Source: OECD (2018[25]), *OECD Regions and Cities at a Glance 2018*, https://dx.doi.org/10.1787/reg_cit_glance-2018-en; Groningen Seaports (2018[23]), "The Northern Netherlands aims to be Europe's most sustainable industrial area by 2030", https://www.groningen-seaports.com/en/nieuws/the-northern-netherlands-aims-to-be-europes-most-sustainable-industrial-area-by-2030/ (accessed on 30 April 2019).

Groningen is the only city in the Northern Netherlands region expecting population growth in the next two decades. The population in the city of Groningen grew 12% from 2004 to 2018. It is foreseen to grow within the next 15 years from approximately 230 000 in 2018 to almost 250 000 (Figure 1.4). Surrounded by a mainly rural region in which the majority of the municipalities are experiencing population decline, the average annual population growth is expected to be 1.3% from 2018 to 2023 and 0.6% from 2024 to 2038 (Groningen Municipality, 2018[24]). Population growth generates the need for new houses by 2030 (20 000) that can be potentially built according to circular principles. The municipality aims to put in place the necessary conditions to create 5 000 new jobs in the next few years by linking the health, information and communications technology (ICT), energy and creative industries to the circular economy. Also, more circularity can be introduced in daily production and consumption activities, from retail to mobility, while contributing to reaching two additional long-term objectives set by the municipality: to become CO2 neutral by 2035 and to separate and reuse all waste by 2030.

Population growth and the increasing number of students are the main drivers of Groningen's demographic changes. The actual birth surplus will continue during the 2018-38 period while mortality will simultaneously increase at a faster pace due to population ageing. In the next 2 decades, the city expects, on average, an inflow of nearly 20 800 immigrants per year (mostly students) and an annual net migrant population surplus of 1 000 people. The main cause of this trend is the continuous inflow and outflow of foreign students. In 2018, the number of students enrolling at the University of Groningen increased by 20%. In the coming years, the presence of foreign European students is expected to double, while the presence of non-EU students will grow by 30%. Nonetheless, almost 3 500 students, aged between 25 and 30 years old, leave the city after finishing their studies, reducing the net population balance (Figure 1.5). In 2017, only 28% of international students remained in the city after finishing their studies. However, to reverse this trend, the city is putting in place several initiatives, such as communication campaigns to showcase the job opportunities available to stay in the city after graduation (Groningen Municipality, 2017[26]; Groningen Municipality, 2018[24]).

Figure 1.4. Population trends in Groningen, Netherlands, 2008-38

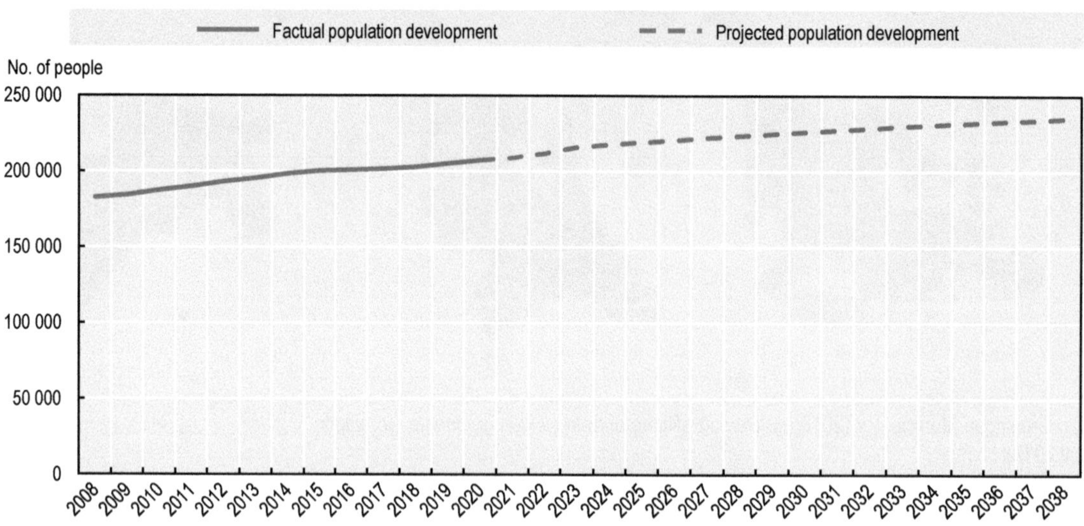

Source: Groningen Municipality (2018[24]), *Demografische ontwikkelingen gemeente Groningen*, https://oisgroningen.nl/bevolkingsprognose-gemeente-groningen-2008-tot-2038/ (accessed on 30 April 2019).

Figure 1.5. Net migration rate in Groningen, Netherlands, 2008-17

25-30 year-olds

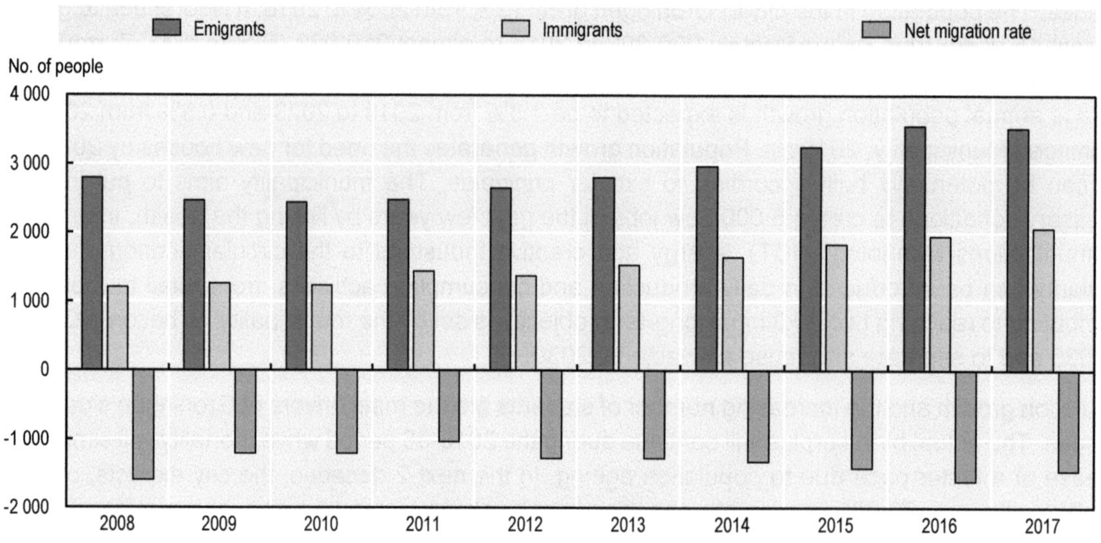

Source: Groningen Municipality (2018[24]), *Demografische ontwikkelingen gemeente Groningen*, https://oisgroningen.nl/bevolkingsprognose-gemeente-groningen-2008-tot-2038/ (accessed on 30 April 2019).

The population group older than 65 is expected to double by 2038. Within 2 decades, the population group aged 65 or higher is expected to experience the highest growth compared to 2018, doubling in size, while the population group aged 25 to 39 will grow by 20%. (Figure 1.6) (Groningen Municipality, 2018[24]). These figures express two contrasting trends affecting the city: an important share of the youth population that does not settle in Groningen after finishing studies and, at the same time, a sustained increase in the senior population.

Figure 1.6. Population trends in Groningen, Netherlands, to 2038, by age group

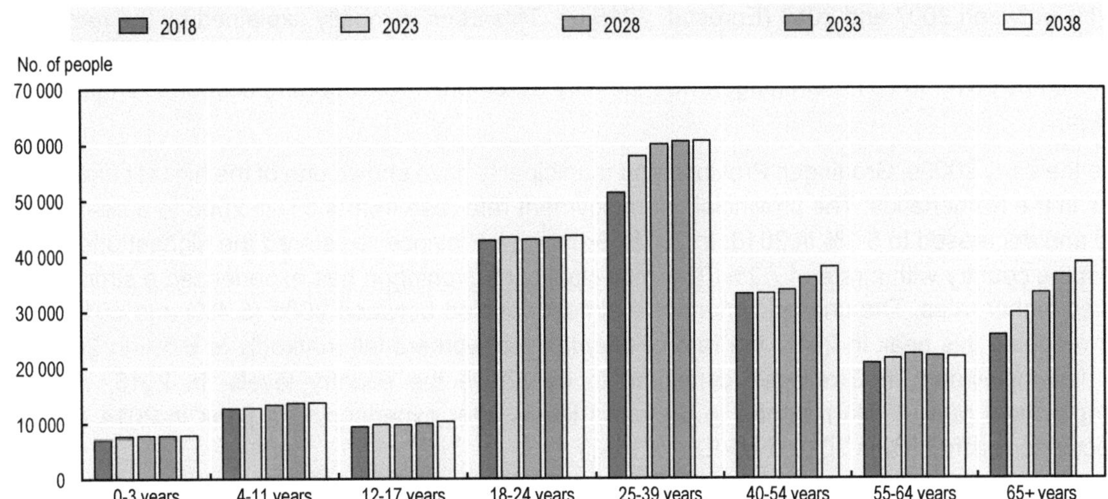

Source: Groningen Municipality (2018[24]), *Demografische ontwikkelingen gemeente Groningen*, https://oisgroningen.nl/bevolkingsprognose-gemeente-groningen-2008-tot-2038/ (accessed on 30 April 2019).

The expected population growth will require an expansion of the housing stock. The city government plans to build 20 000 new houses by 2030. This plan is considered a necessary condition to meet the growing population of 230 000 inhabitants by that time (Groningen Municipality, 2018[24]). This represents an opportunity for the city to ensure that the new housing stock is built in a circular way, advancing in the reduction of the city's carbon footprint (see next section). In November 2018, the city was designated a European "lighthouse city"[7] aiming to become a Smart Zero CO2 City in the next two decades.

Groningen is a digital city and knowledge hub for the region. The city's research facilities are increasingly specialising in cyber safety, big data and blockchain. Since 2017, Groningen has been hosting the largest international blockchain hackathon, gathering 6 000+ participants from all over the world. The University of Groningen hosts the Digital Business Centre to support new talents and entrepreneurs in starting their digital company. It also allows connections with big firms already located in the city, such as Google and IBM (University of Groningen, 2019[27]). The growing digital sector specialisation led to defining Groningen as the "new silicon valley" (DVHN, 2018[28]). The city ranks second for the number of online companies in the Netherlands and it is the country's 2nd Internet city, currently rolling out 5G technology.[8]

There is a vibrant business and innovation scene. A total of 20 000 companies (e.g. in agro-food, energy, healthcare, chemical industry and digital society sectors) are based in Groningen and 400 of them are international firms. The city has been classified as the 2nd tech city in the Netherlands during the last 5 years based on the presence of a high number of fast-growing start-ups. In 2018, Groningen hosted 8 of the 50 fastest-growing start-ups only surpassed by Amsterdam (Deloitte Fast50, 2018[29]). The city's economy is driven by the education, care and services sectors, employing a total of 145 000 people (Groningen Municipality, 2017[30]). The firm creation rate in the Groningen Province stands between 10% and 12% and the number of patents registered per million inhabitants is between 70 and 140. Both figures match Amsterdam's levels (OECD, 2018[25]). In the Groningen Province, the main activities are related to the industry, business sector, mineral extraction and ICT. Groningen Province represents almost 4% of the Dutch GDP (EC, 2019[31]). On the other hand, the contribution of the provinces of Drenthe and Friesland to the national GDP and labour productivity growth are among the lowest in the country (OECD, 2016[32]).

The economic activity in the Northern Netherlands region has been decreasing markedly in the last decade but it is expected to recover gradually. Between 2012 and 2015, the Northern Netherlands region was one of the 6 EU regions that suffered the biggest contraction in economic activities from a total of 38 regions analysed. The regional GDP decreased at an annual average rate of 3.1%, below the Dutch average which increased by 1.5% in the same period (EC, 2019[33]). In Groningen Province, the GDP per capita decreased by 31% between 2007 and 2016 (Eurostat, 2018[34]). This trend is mostly explained by the restrictions on natural gas production applied by the national government from 2013, which led to a 50% reduction in gas extraction by 2017. In 2017, Groningen was the only Dutch province reporting economic shrinkage (CBS, 2018[35]).

Since the early 2000s, Groningen Province and municipality have shown one of the highest unemployment levels in the Netherlands. The provincial unemployment rate rose from 4.5% in 2008 to a peak of 8.5% in 2015 and decreased to 5.1% in 2018. In 2016, Groningen Province registered the highest unemployment rate in the country with a rate of 7.2%. The municipality of Groningen has experienced a similar trend but at even higher rates. The unemployment rate almost doubled between 2008 (5.4%) and 2015 (10.5%).[9] After reaching this peak in 2015, the rate of unemployed workers fell markedly to 6.6% in 2018 (Figure 1.7). Unemployment in Groningen continues to be above the country levels. In 2018, the national unemployment rate (3.8%) returned to pre-crisis levels after experiencing a peak in 2014 (7%) and is expected to reach 3.5% in 2019 (EURES, 2018[36]).

Figure 1.7. Unemployment trends, 2003-18

National, regional, provincial and municipal levels

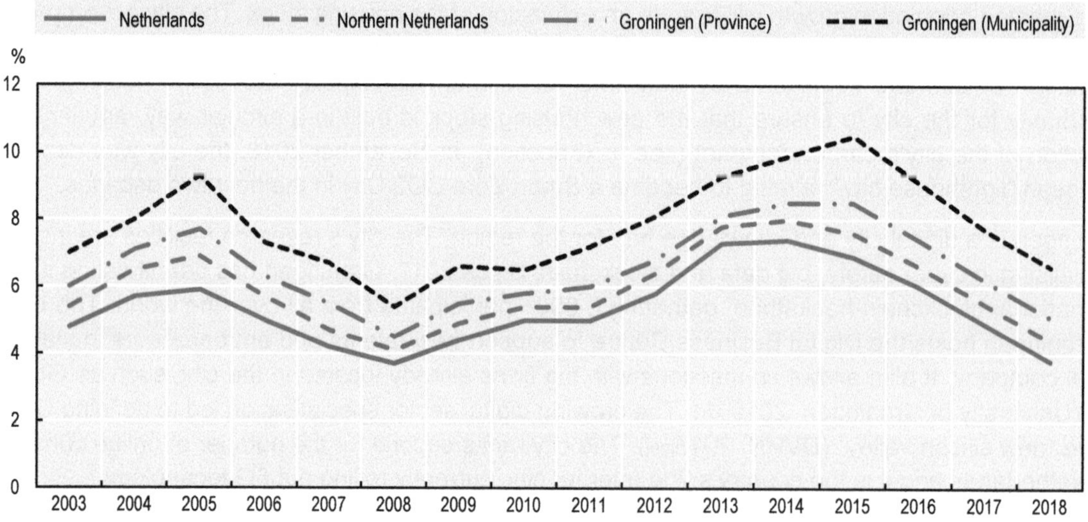

Source: Own elaboration based on CBS (2018[37]), *Arbeidsdeelname; regionale indeling 2018*, https://opendata.cbs.nl/statline#/CBS/nl/ (accessed on 2 May 2019).

The Northern Netherlands region expects employment growth in the coming years. This is mainly due to the creation of an increasing number of vacancies in the technology, engineering and ICT sectors as well as in education, health, transport and logistics. The digital economy is the fastest-growing sector in the region. A total of 7 300 jobs are related to the digital economy and projected to grow in the future, as there is a demand for 400+ ICT jobs to be filled (Groningen Municipality, 2017[38]). Employment is increasing mainly in the private sector, healthcare and temporary employment arrangements. In Groningen, citizens show a low level of satisfaction in relation to employment (27%) and housing (47%), compared with health services (95%), public spaces (94%) and education services (88%), which instead score very high (Eurostat, 2019[22]). It is not yet clear exactly how the transition towards a circular economy will affect the employment rate by sector in the city. However, the municipality aims to put in place the necessary conditions to create 5 000 new jobs in the next few years linking the health, ICT, energy and creative industries to the circular economy. Questions remain on the type of skills to be developed for future jobs in the circular economy. Both low- and high-skilled jobs will be needed, stimulating the demand for new training and educational programmes.

Overview of environmental data and trends

Groningen is taking action towards reaching ambitious environmental goals, such as energy neutrality. Following the municipality's goal of becoming energy neutral by 2035, new forms of energy have recently been tested. The production of green electricity, from solar and wind sources, the advances in renewable heating (from biomass, soil energy and biogas) and hydrogen are examples of the new energy mix that the city aims to achieve. In 2017, the city accounted for a share of 5.9% renewable energy out of the total energy production, compared to the national average of 6.6% (CO_2 Monitor Groningen, 2018[39]). The municipality plans to increase the renewable energy production share to 9.4% by 2023 (Groningen Municipality, 2015[40]). The city is paying specific attention to the energy transition following the Dutch national cabinet's decision to phase out gas production by 2022, for which the region has been the major supplier in the country for the last 60 years (see section on energy transition).

The phasing out of natural gas extraction is creating opportunities for renewable energy in the region. For the past 60 years, the North Netherlands region has been a major supplier of natural gas. In 2015, 56% of the total gas production in the Netherlands was generated in the Groningen field (Evert van de Graaff, van Geuns and Boersma, 2018[41]). However, since 2013, natural gas extraction has been reduced by 50%. In 2018, the Dutch national cabinet decided to scale back gas production and, for the first time, the Netherlands became a net importer of natural gas (CBS, 2018[35]). This decision came after pressing requests from the population living near the gas fields and suffering earthquakes induced by the extraction of natural gas (Bourne et al., 2014[42]; Grasso and Wittlinger, 1990[43]; Nederlandse Aardolie Maatschappij BV, 2013[44]; Wetmiller, 1986[45]). The 3.6-magnitude earthquake in 2012 near Huizinge led to a 50% reduction in natural gas extraction. However, only after the 3.4-magnitude episode in 2018 did the government decide on phasing out by 2022. There is a momentum for the city of Groningen and for the entire region to rethink their role as key players in the energy sector. As such, new forms of energy (e.g. hydrogen, biomass) have been tested in recent years (Groningen Municipality, 2015[40]).

Groningen is transitioning from being a major player in the natural gas sector to becoming a green energy front-runner. The municipality launched the "Groningen Energises" Programme 2015-18 in order to accelerate the city's energy transition from a historic natural gas producer to a "green energy city" focusing on energy transition and bio-based economy opportunities (Groningen Municipality, 2015[40]). The city also recently published the roadmap "Groningen CO2 Neutral 2035. Strategy 2023 and final image 2035" towards becoming CO2 neutral by 2035 (Groningen Municipality, 2018[46]). To secure heat demand during the energy transition, the municipality developed a map that establishes which city districts will become totally electric, which areas will receive energy through a heat network and which neighbourhoods will experience hybrid solutions (a combination of electricity and green gas). By 2035, according to the roadmap's goals, the city will replace gas, gasoline and diesel as energy sources by using sustainably generated electricity (especially produced from wind and solar sources). The industry sector will use sustainable electricity in at least half of the heating processes involved in the production chains (the remaining required energy will be provided by biogas and green gas); and all cars will be fossil-free and emission-free (1/3 electric, 1/3 hydrogen, 1/3 biofuel) (Groningen Municipality, 2018[46]). The following alternative energy sources are used or will be in the future:

- **Hydrogen**: Groningen is the only city in the region that foresees hydrogen in its future energy plans. The New Energy Coalition, a group created in 2018, formed by knowledge and educational institutions, key companies working on the energy transition and governments, favours the experimentation with hydrogen, because of its capacity to store energy and the potential of using the existing natural gas infrastructure. In 2019, the city developed a New Economic Plan for "green hydrogen". "Green hydrogen" is foreseen to be produced using electricity from renewable sources (electrolysis of water). Some issues to be addressed include the requirement of high levels of electricity to generate hydrogen, in addition to safety and infrastructural aspects.

- **Solar**: A total of 700 000 solar panels are projected to be installed in Groningen by 2023. Solar energy has been increasing at the household level: in 2017, in the city, almost 30 000 solar panels were installed in private houses (46% more than in 2016). That same year, 3 parks accounted for more than 50 000 panels: Vierverlaten near Hoogkerk (7 777), Woldjerspoor (43 000) and Zernike (1 700) (Groninger Internet Courant, 2018[47]).

- **Wind**: A total of 274 wind turbines produce energy in the Groningen province (34 at Delfzijl; 90 at Eemshaven and 150 at the Gemini offshore wind farm). The Gemini offshore wind project, one of the largest offshore wind farms in the world, is located 85 km away from the coast in the North Sea with a total capacity of 600 megawatts, meeting the annual energy needs of 1.5 million people and reducing the annual CO2 emissions of the Netherlands by 1.25 million tonnes (Northland Power, 2019[48]). The goal of the region is to produce 855.5 MW by 2020. At the same time, wind energy has generated some resistance to the installation of windmill parks from communities in different regions of the Netherlands.

Green electricity production has grown in the last five years, although it is still relatively low. The production of green electricity (from solar and wind sources) within the municipality grew by 500% in 5 years (from 5 million kWh in 2012 to 27.4 million kWh in 2017) (Figure 1.8). The production in 2017 alone represented the electricity required by 12 000 households, avoiding 12 kilotonnes (kt) of CO2 emissions (CO$_2$ Monitor Groningen, 2018[39]). While solar energy production has grown steadily between 2012 and 2017, wind energy has declined during the same period. This can partly be explained by the existence of subsidies on solar energy, conflicts driven by land property and the so-called "Not In My Backyard" (NIMBY) attitude regarding the installation of wind energy turbines.

Figure 1.8. Green electricity production in Groningen, Netherlands, 2012-17

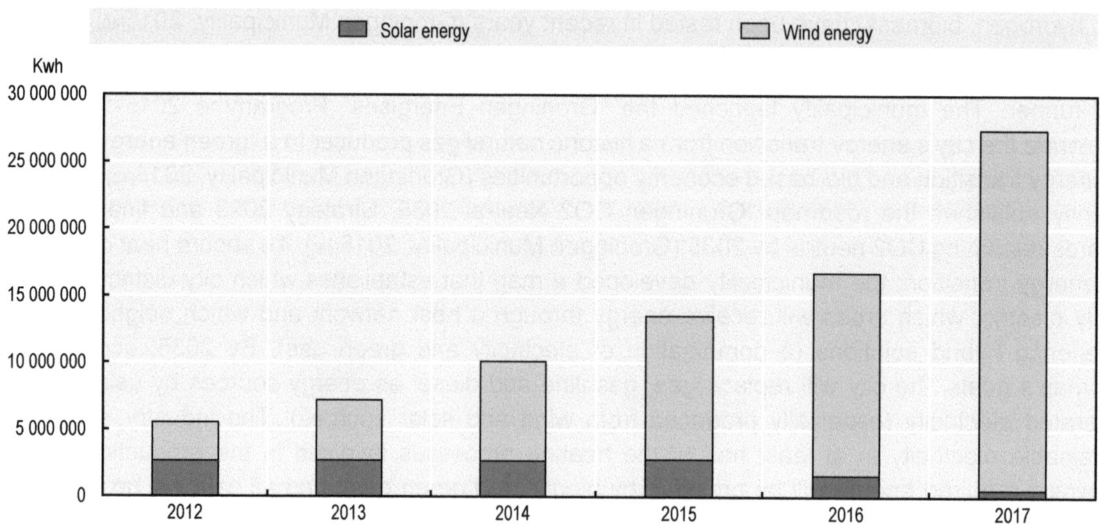

Source: Own elaboration based on CO2 Monitor Groningen (2018[39]), *CO₂ Monitor Groningen*, https://www.groningenco2neutraal.nl/ (accessed on 29 April 2019).

Renewable heating consumption has tripled in five years and this trend is expecting to increase. The total production of renewable heating in 2017 was 327 TJ, almost 3 times the production registered in 2012 (approximately 110 TJ; Figure 1.9). This volume of production provided heating to 8 700 households and prevented 18.3 kt of CO2 emission.[10] Biomass, coming from wood residues, manure and waste from the food processing industry, along with soil energy are the most common types of heating sources in Groningen. The Netherlands is at the bottom of a ranking of a group of 34 EU member countries in terms of the share of renewable energy gross final energy production (European Environment Agency, 2018[49]).

Figure 1.9. Renewable heating consumption in Groningen, Netherlands, 2013-17

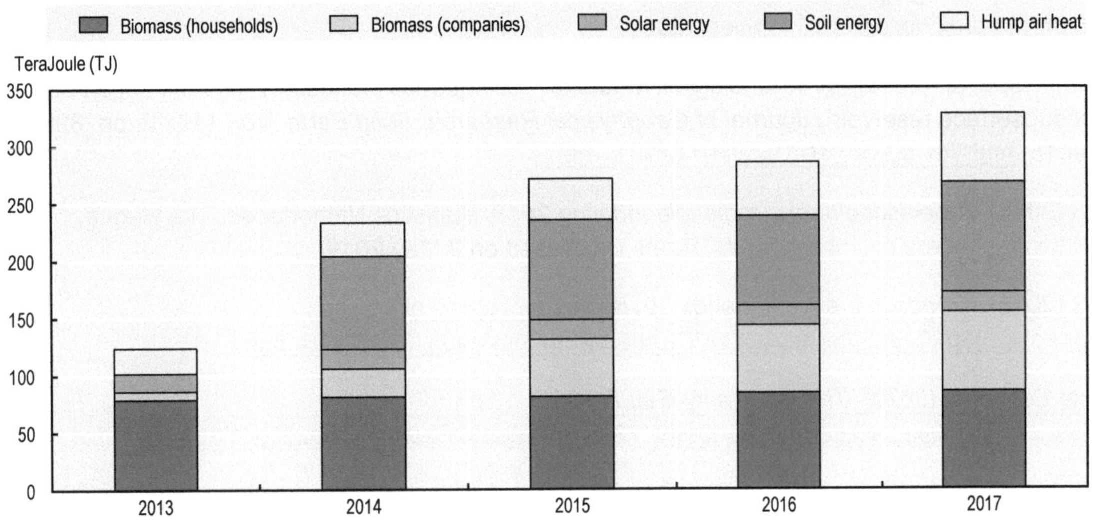

Source: Own elaboration based on CO₂ Monitor Groningen (2018[39]), *CO₂-Monitor Groningen*, https://www.groningenco2neutraal.nl/ (accessed on 29 April 2019).

References

5Groningen (2019), *Homepage*, http://www.5groningen.nl/en (accessed on 30 April 2019).   [51]

Accenture (2015), "The circular economy could unlock $4.5 trillion of economic growth", https://newsroom.accenture.com/news/the-circular-economy-could-unlock-4-5-trillion-of-economic-growth-finds-new-book-by-accenture.htm (accessed on 21 February 2020).   [14]

Blomsma, F. and G. Brennan (2017), "The emergence of circular economy: A new framing around prolonging resource productivity", *Journal of Industrial Ecology*, Vol. 21/3, pp. 603-614, http://dx.doi.org/10.1111/jiec.12603.   [8]

Bourne, S. et al. (2014), "A seismological model for earthquakes induced by fluid extraction from a subsurface reservoir", *Journal of Geophysical Research: Solid Earth*, Vol. 119/12, pp. 8991-9015, http://dx.doi.org/10.1002/2014JB011663.   [41]

CBS (2018), *Arbeidsdeelname; regionale indeling 2018*, Statistics Netherlands, The Hague, https://opendata.cbs.nl/statline#/CBS/nl/ (accessed on 2 May 2019).   [36]

CBS (2018), *Trends in the Netherlands 2018*, http://www.cbs.nl/-/media/_pdf/2018/26/trends%20in%20the%20netherlands_2018_web.pdf.   [34]

Circle Economy (2020), *The Circularity Gap Report*, https://docs.wixstatic.com/ugd/ad6e59_733a71635ad946bc9902dbdc52217018.pdf.   [17]

City of Groningen (2018), *CO$_2$-monitor Groningen*, https://www.groningenco2neutraal.nl/co2-monitor (accessed on 8 November 2019).   [49]

City of Groningen (2015), *Groningen Cycling Strategy 2015-2025*, https://groningenfietsstad.nl/friksbeheer/wp-content/uploads/2016/05/Groningen_CycleCity_Strategy_2015-2025.pdf (accessed on 2 May 2019).   [20]

CO$_2$ Monitor Groningen (2018), *CO$_2$-Monitor Groningen*, https://www.groningenco2neutraal.nl/ (accessed on 29 April 2019).   [38]

Deloitte Fast50 (2018), "8 companies from Groningen in the Deloitte Fast50 › Founded in Groningen", https://www.foundedingroningen.com/news/8-companies-from-groningen-in-the-deloitte-fast50 (accessed on 30 April 2019).   [29]

DVHN (2018), "Noord-Nederland ontpopt zich tot het nieuwe Silicon Valley", https://www.dvhn.nl/extra/Noord-Nederland-ontpopt-zich-tot-het-nieuwe-Silicon-Valley-23901389.html (accessed on 30 April 2019).   [28]

EC (2019), *Province of Groningen - Internal Market, Industry, Entrepreneurship and SMES*, European Commission, https://ec.europa.eu/growth/tools-databases/regional-innovation-monitor/base-profile/province-groningen (accessed on 29 April 2019).   [31]

EC (2015), *Closing the Loop – An EU Action Plan for the Circular Economy*, European Commission, https://eur-lex.europa.eu/legal-content/EN/TXT/HTML/?uri=CELEX:52015DC0614&from=EN (accessed on 21 February 2020).   [9]

Economic Board Groningen (2019), *Homepage*, https://www.economicboardgroningen.nl/nl [52]
(accessed on 30 April 2019).

EEA (2016), *Environmental Indicator Report 2016 — In Support to the Monitoring of the 7th* [16]
Environment Action Programme, European Environment Agency,
https://www.eea.europa.eu//publications/environmental-indicator-report-2016 (accessed on
21 February 2020).

Ekins, P., Domenech, T., Drummond, P., Bleischwitz, R., Hughes, N. and Lotti, L. (2019), "The [12]
circular economy: What, why, how and where", Background paper for an OECD/EC
Workshop on 5 July 2019 within the workshop series "Managing environmental and energy
transitions for regions and cities", Paris.

Ellen MacArthur Foundation (2019), *Cities and Circular Economy for Food.* [7]

Ellen MacArthur Foundation (2018), *What is a Circular Economy?*, [10]
https://www.ellenmacarthurfoundation.org/circular-economy/concept (accessed on
21 February 2020).

EURES (2018), *Labour Market Information - Noord-Nederland*, European Commission, [35]
https://ec.europa.eu/eures/main.jsp?catId=7437&lmi=Y&acro=lmi&lang=en&recordLang=en&
parentId=&countryId=NL®ionId=NL0&nuts2Code=%20&nuts3Code=null&mode=shortage
s®ionName=Noord-Nederland (accessed on 30 April 2019).

European Environment Agency (2018), *Renewable Energy Sources: Setting the Scene*, Annual [48]
Indicator Report Series (AIRS).

Eurostat (2019), *Urban Europe - Statistics on Cities, Towns and Suburbs - Satisfaction and* [22]
Quality of Life in Cities, Statistics Explained, https://ec.europa.eu/eurostat/ (accessed on
29 April 2019).

Eurostat (2018), *Change of Gross Domestic Product (GDP) per Inhabitant in Purchasing Power* [33]
Standards (PPS) in Relation to the EU-28 Average, By NUTS 2 Regions, 2007–2015
(Percentage Points Difference between 2007 and 2015), Statistics Explained,
https://ec.europa.eu/eurostat/ (accessed on 30 April 2019).

Evert van de Graaff, W., L. van Geuns and T. Boersma (2018), "The termination of Groningen [40]
gas production production - Background and next steps", Columbia SIPA Center on Global
Energy Policy,
https://energypolicy.columbia.edu/sites/default/files/pictures/CGEP_Groningen-
Commentary_072518_0.pdf (accessed on 29 April 2019).

Grasso, J. and G. Wittlinger (1990), "Ten years of seismic monitoring over a gas field", *Bulletin of* [42]
the Seismological Society of America, https://pubs.geoscienceworld.org/ssa/bssa/article-
abstract/80/2/450/102493/ten-years-of-seismic-monitoring-over-a-gas-
field?redirectedFrom=fulltext (accessed on 30 April 2019).

Groningen Municipality (2018), *Council Proposal: Groningen Circular.* [19]

Groningen Municipality (2018), *Demografische ontwikkelingen gemeente Groningen*, [24]
https://oisgroningen.nl/bevolkingsprognose-gemeente-groningen-2008-tot-2038/ (accessed
on 30 April 2019).

Groningen Municipality (2018), *Routekaart Groningen CO2-Neutraal 2035. Strategie 2023 en Eindbeeld 2035*, https://gemeente.groningen.nl/sites/default/files/Routekaart-Groningen-Energie-%28CO2---neutraal%29.pdf (accessed on 6 June 2019). [45]

Groningen Municipality (2017), *Employment and Economy*, https://oisgroningen.nl/wp-content/uploads/2019/10/thema05-werk-economie.pdf (accessed on 2 May 2019). [30]

Groningen Municipality (2017), *Groningen City Monitor - Students*, http://www.groningencitymonitor.nl/en/the-people/students (accessed on 2 May 2019). [21]

Groningen Municipality (2017), *International Groningen - How Can We Make Groningen More Welcoming?*, https://gemeente.groningen.nl/sites/default/files/Welkomstbeleid%20International%20Groningen.pdf (accessed on 30 April 2019). [26]

Groningen Municipality (2017), *Statistical Overview of the Municipality of Groningen*, https://os-groningen.nl/wp-content/uploads/2017/04/thema06-werkloosheid.pdf (accessed on 30 April 2019). [37]

Groningen Municipality (2015), *Groningen Energizes Programme 2015-2018*, https://gemeente.groningen.nl/sites/default/files/Groningen%20energizes.pdf (accessed on 30 April 2019). [39]

Groningen Seaports (2018), "The Northern Netherlands aims to be Europe's most sustainable industrial area by 2030", https://www.groningen-seaports.com/en/nieuws/the-northern-netherlands-aims-to-be-europes-most-sustainable-industrial-area-by-2030/ (accessed on 30 April 2019). [23]

Groninger Internet Courant (2018), "Aantal Groningse zonnepanelen in jaar tijd verdubbeld", Groninger Internet Courant, https://www.gic.nl/innovatie/aantal-zonnepanelen-in-jaar-tijd-verdubbeld (accessed on 29 April 2019). [46]

IEA (2016), "Cities are in the frontline for cutting carbon emissions", https://www.iea.org/news/cities-are-in-the-frontline-for-cutting-carbon-emissions-new-iea-report-finds (accessed on 21 February 2020). [2]

Kirchherr, J., D. Reike and M. Hekkert (2017), *Conceptualizing the Circular Economy: An Analysis of 114 Definitions*, Elsevier B.V., http://dx.doi.org/10.1016/j.resconrec.2017.09.005. [11]

McKinsey Centre for Business and Environment (2016), *Growth Within: A Circular Economy Vision for a Competitive Europe*. [15]

Nederlandse Aardolie Maatschappij BV (2013), *A Technical Addendum to the Winningsplan Groningen 2013: Subsidence, Induced Earthquakes and Seismic Hazard Analysis in the Groningen Field*, https://www.tweedekamer.nl/downloads/document?id=4ce3b996-fcb3-4d7b-9fd6-89be7fa10570&title=Technical%20Addendum%20to%20the%20Winningsplan%20Groningen%202013.%20Subsidence%2C%20Induced%20Earthquakes%20and%20Seismic%20Hazard%20Analysis%20in%20the%20Groning (accessed on 30 April 2019). [43]

Northland Power (2019), *Gemini (Offshore Wind)*, https://www.northlandpower.com/What-We-Do/Operating-Assets/Wind/Gemini.aspx (accessed on 27 November 2019). [47]

OCDE (2012), *OECD Environmental Outlook to 2050: The Consequences of Inaction*, OECD Publishing, Paris, https://doi.org/10.1787/9789264122246-en. [4]

OECD (2019), *Global Material Resources Outlook to 2060: Economic Drivers and Environmental Consequences*, OECD Publishing, Paris, https://dx.doi.org/10.1787/9789264307452-en. [13]

OECD (2019), *OECD Survey on the Circular Economy in Cities and Regions*, OECD, Paris. [18]

OECD (2018), *OECD Regions and Cities at a Glance 2018*, OECD Publishing, Paris, https://dx.doi.org/10.1787/reg_cit_glance-2018-en. [25]

OECD (2016), *OECD Regional Outlook 2016: Productive Regions for Inclusive Societies*, OECD Publishing, Paris, http://dx.doi.org/10.1787/9789264260245-en (accessed on 22 July 2019). [32]

OECD (2015), *OECD Regional Statistics*, OECD, Paris, https://doi.org/10.1787/region-data-en. [53]

OECD (2012), *Functional urban areas by country - OECD*, https://www.oecd.org/cfe/regional-policy/functionalurbanareasbycountry.htm (accessed on 24 February 2020). [54]

SmartEnCity (2019), *SmartEnCity.eu*, https://smartencity.eu/about/ (accessed on 30 April 2019). [50]

UN (2018), "68% of the world population projected to live in urban areas by 2050", United Nations, http://www.un.org/development/desa/en/news/population/2018-revision-of-world-urbanization-prospects.html (accessed on 6 November 2019). [1]

UNEP (2013), *UNEP-DTIE Sustainable Consumption and Production Branch*. [5]

UNEP/IWSA (2015), *Global Waste Management Outlook*. [6]

University of Groningen (2019), *Groningen Digital Business Centre*, https://www.rug.nl/gdbc/over-ons/ (accessed on 27 November 2019). [27]

Wetmiller, R. (1986), "Earthquakes near Rocky Mountain House, Alberta, and their relationship to gas production facilities", *Canadian Journal of Earth Sciences*, Vol. 23/2, pp. 172-181, http://dx.doi.org/10.1139/e86-020. [44]

World Bank (2010), *World Development Report 2010*, World Bank, http://dx.doi.org/10.1596/978-0-8213-7987-5. [3]

Notes

[1] Concentrations in air pollutants refer in particular to Particulate Matter (PM10).

[2] Amec Foster Wheeler - See focus area profiles in this document: https://www.lwarb.gov.uk/wp-content/uploads/2015/12/LWARB-circular-economy-report_web_09.12.15.pdf (pp. 20-30) (2015).

[3] For more information, see https://www.paris.fr/economiecirculaire.

[4] There are 380 municipalities in the Netherlands. The number has been reducing over the past years due to a merging of small municipalities in order to improve policymaking and service delivery.

[5] A functional urban area (FUA) consists of a densely inhabited city and of a surrounding area (commuting zone) whose labour market is highly integrated with the city (OECD, 2012[55]).

[6] A frontier region is defined as the top 10% of regions in GDP per employee. These are regions with the highest GDP per employee until the equivalent of 10% of national employment is reached (OECD, 2015[54]).

[7] "Lighthouse" cities are part of the EU Horizon 2020 project SmartEnCity which aims to develop a highly adaptable and replicable systemic approach for transforming European cities into sustainable, smart and resource-efficient urban environments. Other cities involved in the project are: Sonderborg in Denmark, Tartu in Estonia and Vitoria-Gasteiz in Spain (SmartEnCity, 2019[51]).

[8] Launched in 2017 by the Economic Board Groningen (EBG), 5Groningen is an initiative by which entrepreneurs and non-profit organisations test 5G applications in five specific sectors: health, energy, traffic, agriculture and living environment. These pilot experiences vary from 5G applications for use in arable and livestock farming in north Groningen, to solutions for the ageing population (5Groningen Website (2019[52]); Economic Board Groningen Website (2019[53]).

[9] Partially, the increase in unemployment between 2013 and 2015 can be attributed to administrative matters. Until 2013, people receiving unemployment benefits were responsible for extending their registration before the Employee Insurance Schemes Implementing Body (*Uitvoeringsinstituut Werknemersverzekeringen*, UWV) and sometimes failed to do it. After 2013, the municipal government started to monitor this issue resulting in a partly artificial increase in the number of unemployment benefits beneficiaries (Groningen Municipality, 2017[38]).

[10] A kilotonne (kt) is a mass unit (1 000 tonnes or 1 million kilograms).

2 Assessing and unlocking the circular economy in Groningen, Netherlands

This chapter details the main components of the existing circular economy strategies and initiatives promoted by the Dutch Government, the Northern Netherlands region, the provinces and the city of Groningen, Netherlands. The chapter also identifies actors, policies and co-operation tools across urban and rural areas that can foster the circular economy. Finally, it describes the main challenges that the city of Groningen is facing in its transition from a linear to a circular economy.

An ongoing agenda on the circular economy at the national level

In 2016, the Dutch national government set a circular economy strategy, which provides goals, inspiration and ambitions to local governments. The aim of the national strategy is to achieve a waste-free economy by 2050. It outlines a vision of a future-proof, sustainable economy for current and future generations. According to the Netherlands Organisation for Applied Scientific Research (*Nederlandse Organisatie voor toegepastnatuurwetenschappelijk Onderzoek,* TNO), the circular economy can generate EUR 7.3 billion within the sectors involved and up to 54 000 jobs, while the use of raw material can be reduced of 100 megatonnes (one-quarter of the Dutch annual import of raw material). The strategy is based on five priorities: biomass and food; plastics; the manufacturing industry; the construction sector; and consumer goods. Adequate regulation, finance and knowledge will help achieve the objective of no waste by 2050. This implies making the best use of raw material, replacing fossil-based materials with sustainable and renewable ones and designing products that can last in time (Ministry of Infrastructure and the Environment/Ministry of Economic Affairs, 2016[1]).

The national government has also made available funds to implement circular economy projects. Funds are linked to the envelope of EUR 300 million that the government makes available annually for climate-related actions. Subnational governments have access to this envelope. At the same time, the Ministry of Infrastructure has allocated EUR 40 million to fund circular economy-related projects in 2019 and 2020, while national regional strategies and SDG implementation programmes also provide financial opportunities to promote the circular economy transition (Netherlands Enterprise Agency, 2019[2]). Businesses and local governments can present projects eligible for national subsidies at the National Enterprise Agency (*Rijksdienst voor Ondernemend Nederland*), although conditions for applying are still to be clarified.

Circular initiatives at the subnational level

The Northern Netherlands region carried out a material flow analysis to identify priority areas for the circular economy. The Northern Netherlands region is one of the six top European regions in the bio-based economy according to the European Union (EC, 2019[3]). About 70% of the land in the region is devoted to agricultural production. As such, there is a high likelihood of transforming agricultural waste into biomass. In 2018, Northern Netherlands commissioned a material flow analysis to better understand the input and output of materials within the region. Four sectors were identified as key for the circular economy: construction, waste, chemistry and agro-food (Metabolic, 2018[4]). The study concluded that, although the perspectives for a circular economy in the three northern provinces, including Groningen, are favourable, there are financial and regulatory bottlenecks to take into account, which are outside the direct sphere of influence of the provinces and the municipalities. Therefore, co-ordination with the national government is needed.

Each province made steps towards the circular economy transition. The province of Friesland launched Circular Friesland, an association of public and private partners, to put in place a number of projects within five main sectors: circular agriculture, circular plastic, organic waste streams, construction and saline agriculture. In collaboration with the national government and the Waste Fund, the province of Friesland launched in 2018 a national test centre for plastics, in order to improve techniques of sorting, recycling and reusing plastic packaging. The centre organises awareness-raising activities on the circular economy. The province of Drenthe plans to use organic materials for plastic production, create a research institution focused on geothermal heating and develop greener energy sources as hydrogen and biogas. The province of Groningen focuses on green chemistry and energy in combination with agro-industry for a future circular economy strategy. Each province could maximise efforts and impacts by being aware of initiatives in other provinces, co-ordinating efforts and learning from one another. Inhibiting factors for collaboration can be related to different political priorities.

Circular economy initiatives in Groningen, Netherlands

The City Council proposal for a Circular Groningen identified three priority areas. In 2018, the council instructed the board to develop a sustainable and circular vision for the city, by co-ordinating the already existing initiatives linked to the circular economy. It identified three priority areas (Groningen Municipality, 2018[5]):

- **Public procurement**: As a means to influence the business community towards circular practices, for example in service provision and in the building sector.
- **Waste**: As an opportunity to re-think the processing of the waste streams towards increased separation and recycling, jointly with the termination of the contract with the waste company in 2022 and with the objective of the city to become waste neutral[1] by 2030.
- **Knowledge**: To establish connections with knowledge networks and create platforms amongst the private, public and not-for-profit sectors.

Referring to the three priority areas identified by the municipal council, a series of existing and planned activities focus on public procurement, waste and knowledge. They are reported in Table 2.1.

Table 2.1. Circular economy activities in Groningen, Netherlands

Sector	Activity	Description	Status
Knowledge and awareness-raising	100x100x100	Awareness campaign challenging 100 households to live 100% waste-free for 100 days. Around 200 households joined. The local television channel followed the participants in a series of programmes.	Delivered in 2017
	Dismissed industrial area as experimentation space	Former sugar factory temporarily hosting 50 initiatives and businesses as a playground for the circular economy.	Ongoing
	The Food Battle	Challenge inviting inhabitants to reduce food waste food. Around 250 households joined.	Delivered in 2017
Procurement	Circular IQ	An online software application for collaboration, data monitoring and analysis that uses simple data to support circular decision-making. It is scheduled to be used for Green Public Procurement.	Not yet in use
	Green Public Procurement	Large scale purchase of circular products used by the municipality in public spaces (e.g. reused materials for constructing bridges decks, waterway timbering and highway fences built using recycled material, waste bins and containers made of circular plastic).	Ongoing
		Purchasing coffee machines, infrastructure projects following circular principles (e.g. reusing, leasing).	Planned
	Green tender office furniture	Replacement of office furniture over ten years in the whole municipality.	Ongoing
	Green Public Procurement training	Eight interactive workshops for purchasing in a circular way: from request and procedure, to measuring and weighing criteria to business models.	Delivered in 2018

Sector	Activity	Description	Status
Waste	Circular Economy Hub	Incubator space for circular small businesses and start-ups, information centre, repair hub and second-hand shops next to the waste delivery station.	Planned
	Groningen designs (*Groningen Ontwerpt*)	Sustainable design to reuse waste streams: new products from waste and residual materials for sale in seven shops in Groningen.	Delivered in 2018
	Reuse	Repair cafes; collection of reusable items and paint for second-hand shops.	Ongoing
	Waste management concession	Inclusion of circular criteria for waste processing for the new waste management concession after the year 2022.	Ongoing
	Waste sorting facility	Waste sorting facility operated by the municipality with the highest possible resource recovery rate and the production of sustainable energy such as green gas.	Ongoing since 1988

Source: OECD (2019[6]) OECD Survey on the Circular Economy in Cities and Regions and Interviews held in the city of Groningen in February 2019.

The city aims to implement Green Public Procurement. City employees are being trained to make this happen through dedicated circular procurement workshops. Green public procurement is being applied to the purchase of a 10-year service of refurbished furniture for the municipality, currently in the tender phase. Since 2018, all public plastic bins must be made of recycled plastics, as established by public procurement requisites.

The city set the goal of becoming waste neutral by 2030, following circular economy principles. Today, 40% of waste is incinerated in Groningen. The city wants to take that rate down to zero by 2030. The goals by 2020 are the following: a maximum of 150 kg of waste for incineration per inhabitant and 65% of waste separated for reuse (100% by 2030). An awareness campaign to communicate regularly on the available options for the separation of waste and to prevent waste production has been put in place. A "circular innovation hub" is scheduled to be developed. The hub will host a bulky waste depot for receiving large reusable household goods (furniture, electrical goods and garden cuttings, among others). The aim is to foster high-end reuse of raw materials such as metal, plastics, beverage cartons and organic waste. A repair café and second-hand shops are also planned to be included in the hub. In addition, an information centre, located in the circular innovation hub, would identify key stakeholders for circular economy activities, possible launching customers and involve designers for product solutions and new business models (Groningen Municipality, 2019[7]).

The city of Groningen supports small- and medium-sized enterprises (SMEs) in the transition towards a circular economy. In 2019, the municipality initiated the "Front Runner Project" (*Koploperproject*) to support SMEs in the implementation of more sustainable and circular business models. During a year, expert advisors produce a baseline measurement analysis of the company; determine its environmental performance and the CO2 footprint, while defining a "sustainability profile". Each company establishes an action plan and a communication strategy based on the recommendations received. The project foresees networking events to promote the exchange of experiences and creates a permanent network among members. Between 8 and 15 companies and SMEs are currently taking part in the project alongside 6 municipalities (Hogeland, Groningen, Oldambt, Stadskanaal, Westerkwartier, Westerwolde), the province of Groningen, co-operatives, banks and educational institutions. Since 2015, six projects have been carried out in the province of Groningen with around 65 participants, with 2 special projects on village houses and the food chain (Koploperproject, 2019[8]).

The analytical framework

The analytical framework used in this report is based on three dimensions that help to identify tailored solutions for cities and regions willing to transition from a linear to a circular economy (Figure 2.1):

- The level of advancement of cities and regions in the transition to a circular economy: Advanced, In progress, Newcomers.
- Tools and instruments for the transition according to the 3Ps Framework: People, Policies and Places.
- Roles of cities and regions to promote, facilitate and enable the circular economy.

According to the level of advancement towards the transition to a circular economy, it is possible to identify three clusters of cities and regions:

- **Advanced**: Cities and regions that have developed and put in place circular economy strategies. These cities show strong innovative initiatives, as well as a firm political will in favour of a circular economy. An important future priority for these cities would be to build metrics for measuring progress and evaluating their policies in place. Brussels and the Flanders region (Belgium), Paris (France), Amsterdam (Netherlands) and London (United Kingdom) belong to this cluster.
- **In progress**: Cities "in progress" are those that are taking actions towards the circular economy, following ad hoc initiatives. Cities or regions in this cluster have recently set specific programmes on the circular economy and/or are starting their implementation. They are less advanced compared to the pioneers, but they have already taken key steps towards a circular economy. This is the case of Rotterdam (Netherlands), the Metropolitan Area of Barcelona (Spain) and Glasgow (United Kingdom), amongst others.
- **Newcomers**: Cities in this cluster recognise the relevance and potential of the circular economy and they are exploring options for implementation. These cities have already achieved good results in waste recycling levels (Oslo, Norway); water-reuse (Granada, Spain); have signed political commitments to advance towards a circular economy (Milan and Prato, Italy); are starting to develop a circular economy strategy (Valladolid, Spain; Umeå, Sweden); or have included the circular economy in broader policy plans (Helsinki and Oulu, Finland). These cities see in the circular economy a means for reducing environmental impacts in cities while increasing attractiveness and competitiveness. The city of Groningen is included in this cluster.

Figure 2.1. OECD analytical framework: Level of advancement, tools and roles

Source: OECD (forthcoming[9]), *The Circular Economy in Cities and Regions*, Synthesis Report, OECD Publishing, Paris.

Each city and region, regardless of their level of advancement, can identify the conditions needed to transition to a circular economy, making sure that *people* are engaged, *policies* are co-ordinated and that linkages across *places* are set to close the loops (3Ps Framework) (OECD, 2016[10]):

- **People**: The circular economy is a shared responsibility across levels of government and stakeholders. As such, it is key to identify the actors that can play a role in the transition and allow the needed cultural shift towards different production and consumption pathways, new business and governance models. For example, the business sector can determine the shift towards new business models (e.g. renting, reusing, sharing, etc.). Citizens, on the other hand, make constant consumption choices and can influence production.

- **Policies**: The circular economy requires a holistic and systemic approach that cuts across sectoral policies. As somebody's waste can be a resource for somebody else, the circular economy provides the opportunity to foster complementarities across policies. The variety of actors, sectors and goals makes the circular economy systemic by nature. It implies a wide policy focus through integration across often siloed policies, from environmental, regional development, agricultural and industrial ones. Identifying these key sectors and possible synergies is the first step to avoid the implementation of fragmented projects over the short-medium run, due to the lack of a systemic approach.

- **Places**: Cities and regions are not isolated ecosystems, but spaces for inflows and outflows of materials, resources and products, in connection with surrounding areas and beyond. Therefore, adopting a functional approach going beyond the administrative boundaries of cities is important for resource management and economic development. Linkages across urban and rural areas (e.g. related to bio-economy, agriculture and forest) are key to promote local production and recycling of organic residuals to be used in proximity of where they are produced, to avoid negative externalities due to transport. At the regional level, loops related to a series of economic activities (e.g. to the bio-economy) can be closed and slowed.

As a result and in accordance with predefined short-, medium- and long-term objectives, cities and regions can play a role as *promoters*, *facilitators* and *enablers* in the transition from a linear to a circular economy. In practice:

- Cities can **promote** the circular economy as illustrated by the roadmaps and strategies set out in cities like Brussels (Belgium), Paris (France), Amsterdam (Netherlands) and London (United Kingdom). These strategies identified priorities, promoted a number of concrete projects and engaged stakeholders.
- Cities can **facilitate** connections across business, citizens and levels of government. They help direct and facilitate contacts, inform about existing projects, provide soft and hard infrastructure for new circular businesses. The city of Phoenix (United States), for example, created together with Arizona State University a Resource Innovation and Solutions Network (RISN) Incubator for accompanying businesses in the shift towards a circular economy. In 2017, the city of Paris, France, launched a circular economy incubator, hosting 19 start-ups.
- Cities can **enable** the circular economy transition to happen by providing the appropriate governance and economic tools. Cities can set up incentives, catalyse funds, adapt regulations, etc. For example, the London Waste and Recycling Board (LWARB) in London (United Kingdom) proposed to develop a venture capital fund, seeking private sector partners to join; the city of Amsterdam (Netherlands) created a revolving sustainability fund for businesses to pay back within 15 years with a very low interest rate.

This analytical framework applied to the case of Groningen, Netherlands, will identify the main opportunities and challenges (Chapter 2), as well as tailored policy recommendations to promote, facilitate and enable the circular economy (Chapter 3).

People and firms: Towards a circular economy ecosystem

Government, business sector and universities could create a circular economy "ecosystem" to allow co-operation and knowledge building. In Groningen, representatives of the universities and the public and private sectors gather together in an organisation called "De Koepel", which meets every three months to identify opportunities for business and collaboration. The meeting held in February 2019 discussed opportunities for a circular economy in Groningen. It concluded with the proposal of creating a circular economy "ecosystem" to allow co-operation and building knowledge, in the same way as for existing ecosystems for the digital economy, energy transition and healthy ageing.[2] Indeed, there is a fertile environment for collaboration in Groningen. For example, the municipality of Groningen, the business association WEST and the province of Groningen co-operate within Campus Groningen, one of the biggest campuses in the Netherlands. Local authorities define the campus as a "model of co-operation" to promote innovation in the energy transition, artificial intelligence, health and, in the future, the circular economy.

The transition towards a circular economy is supported by various public, private and not-for-profit organisations. For example, the business association West, representing more than 300 SMEs and entrepreneurs, brings together SMEs working alongside the local government on waste, energy and bio-economy. These sectors are all relevant within the circular economy approach; therefore, specific initiatives to maximise resource efficiency, reuse resources and prevent waste generation are increasingly foreseen in the future. Private, public and not-for-profit sectors can receive support for building capacities and identifying opportunities for collaboration through the Northern Innovation Circular Economy (NICE) lab, which aims at speeding up the transition from a linear to a circular economy. This initiative gathers 18 organisations, including local governments, SMEs and knowledge institutes. Similarly, associations and non-governmental organisations (NGOs) are raising awareness on circular economy practices and implementing circular economy principles in the food and construction sectors (see section on policies).

The Circular Economy Club is a platform created by local retailers in 2018 to discuss common problems and solutions related to their business activities and following circular economy principles. The club can play a role in connecting the municipality with entrepreneurs and companies to develop a long-term circular economy city-wide vision. Stakeholders are organised in different thematic commissions. One of the commissions focuses on waste management and product distribution. The club is currently dealing with the problem of traffic caused by waste collection in the city centre for a large number of companies. It is trying to find solutions for an emission-free city in liaison with the Waste and Mobility Department of the Municipality.

Policies: Identifying sectors holding potential for the circular economy

All sectors are concerned in a circular economy but some have higher potential. Often the circular economy in cities and regions is seen as a synonymous with municipal waste recycling but it is more than that. Cities and regions in their circular economy strategies have identified key sectors that show the greatest potential in terms of economic, social and environmental benefits. These sectors include built environment, food, water, and textile amongst others. According to local specificities, cities and regions are setting up circular economy initiatives for less traditional sectors, such as fashion and culture.

Making a sector "circular" implies rethinking value chains and production and consumption processes. "Circularity" implies that any output can be an input for something else within and across sectors. It aims to: make products and goods last longer through better design; produce products and goods using secondary and reusable materials and renewable energy while reducing atmospheric emissions; produce and distribute products locally and consume them in a conscious and sustainable manner; and transform waste into a resource (Figure 2.2).

Various sectors can be taken into account when it comes to fostering the transition from a linear to a circular economy in Groningen, Netherlands. According to the results of the *OECD Survey on the Circular Economy in Cities and Regions* (OECD, 2019[6]), the municipality identified the following sectors as of interest for a circular economy strategy in Groningen: waste, mobility, water, energy, food and beverage, sanitation, biomass, construction and demolition and creative industry (Figure 2.3). Below, specific attention will be dedicated to those sectors that more prominently stand out from the discussion with various stakeholders in Groningen. This is key to establish the role of the "do-ers" (e.g. entrepreneurs, SMEs, private companies, CSOs, etc.) in the transition from a linear to a circular economy and foresee coherent policies for the future. Information on the sectors included in other cities' and regions' circular economy initiatives is presented in Table 2.2.

Figure 2.2. Circularity within and across sectors

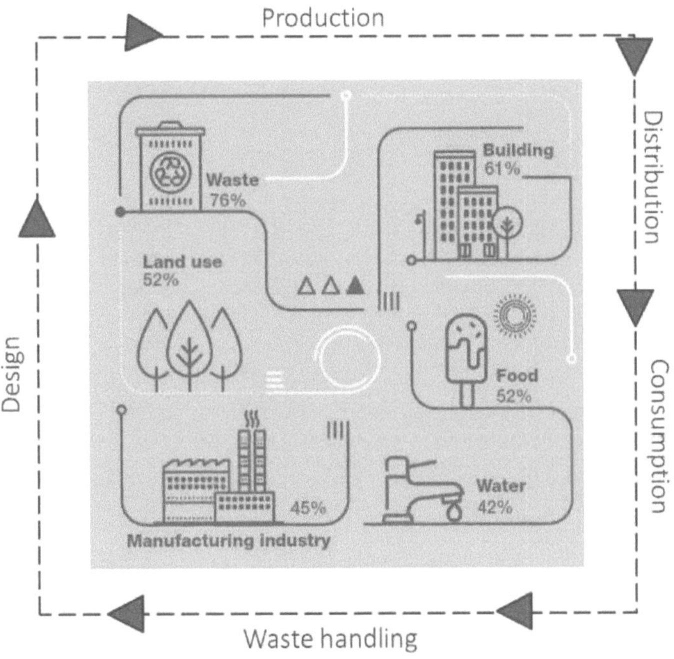

Source: OECD (forthcoming[9]), *The Circular Economy in Cities and Regions*, Synthesis Report, OECD Publishing, Paris.

Figure 2.3. Sectors of interest for a circular economy strategy in Groningen, Netherlands

Source: Own elaboration based on the city of Valladolid's answers to the OECD (2019[6]) OECD Survey on the Circular Economy in Cities and Regions.

Table 2.2. Example of sectors included in circular economy initiatives in cities and regions

City/Region	Initiative	Waste	Construction and demolition	Land use and spatial planning	Food and beverage	Manufacturing industry	Textile	Water and sanitation	Energy	Biomass	Agriculture	Mobility	ICT sector	Forestry	Culture
Amsterdam (Netherlands)	Amsterdam Circular 2020-25	✓	✓	✓	✓	✓	✓	✓	✓	✓	✓	✓	✓		
Barcelona Metropolitan Area (AMB) (Spain)	Circular Economy Promotion Programme AMB Circular (2019)		✓	✓	✓			✓	✓	✓	✓	✓			
Flanders (Belgium)	Circular Flanders (2016)	✓	✓	✓	✓	✓		✓					✓		
Greater Porto Area (Portugal)	LIPOR's commitment to circular economy principles (2018)	✓	✓	✓	✓		✓	✓	✓		✓	✓			
Nantes (France)	Circular Economy Roadmap	✓	✓	✓	✓				✓	✓	✓	✓			
North Karelia (Finland)	CIRCWASTE – Towards Circular Economy in North Karelia	✓	✓	✓	✓	✓		✓	✓	✓	✓	✓		✓	
Paris (France)	Circular Economy Plan of Paris 2017-20	✓	✓	✓					✓	✓					✓
Rotterdam (Netherlands)	Rotterdam Circularity Programme 2019-23	✓	✓	✓	✓	✓		✓		✓	✓				
Scotland (United Kingdom)	Circular Glasgow	✓	✓		✓	✓	✓		✓		✓		✓	✓	
Tilburg (Netherlands)	Tilburg Circular Agenda 2019	✓	✓	✓	✓	✓	✓			✓					
Valladolid (Spain)	Valladolid Circular Economy Roadmap (2017-18)		✓	✓	✓	✓	✓	✓		✓		✓			

Source: OECD (forthcoming[9]), *The Circular Economy in Cities and Regions*, Synthesis Report, OECD Publishing, Paris.

Waste

The city of Groningen is planning to become waste neutral by 2030. The municipality of Groningen is responsible for the municipal and household waste collection. Private companies collect industrial waste. Groningen's household and municipal waste processing takes place at the treatment plant managed by Attero in the city of Wijster (separation and incineration) and Groningen (separation).[1] Separated waste is treated for secondary material production and biomass is processed into biogas. There are different producers of biogas in the city (Attero, RWZI Garmerwolde, Stainkoeln and Suiker Unie) (CO_2 Monitor Groningen, 2018[11]). Today, the biogas production capacity has the potential to provide 17 000 homes with gas. During the summer, when temperatures are higher than 30°C, it could meet the green gas demand of the entire city. Suiker Unie provides 7 000 households with green gas generated from fermented sugar beet residues. Green gas producers call for energy taxes to foster green fuels. The city is also promoting waste prevention campaigns and challenges amongst citizens to reduce waste production (e.g. 100x100x100, Table 2.1). Further actions should be dedicated to the policy options for reducing and securing the safety of industrial and commercial waste. There is little or no incentive for separate collection of industrial waste and for organic collection from restaurants and bars in the city. However, a separate facility is in place for the collection of organic waste.

Food

Minimising food waste and increasing local food production is part of current and future circular activities. The municipality launched "Food Battle Groningen" to raise awareness on reducing food waste (Table 2.1). Local not-for-profit organisations are taking the lead in this sector by pushing the demand towards local food consumption, reducing food waste and promoting urban agriculture. As such, the circular approach, whereby the overall food chain can reduce the production of waste from beginning to end, has the potential to benefit vulnerable social groups by creating job opportunities and engaging communities (Box 2.1). For example, the Toentje Foundation produces honey, food and beer in disadvantaged neighbourhoods. Another example is the Reframe Project[2] in the food chain, bringing together farmers, producers and government since 2015. The idea of the project is to reduce food waste by allocating food leftovers to potential customers as the hospital. The Regional Cooperative of Western Catering,[3] created in 2013, aims to develop new business models rethinking food chains for the next generation of co-operative business and start-ups. Nevertheless, some regulatory and financial barriers inhibit these activities: from legal regulations, preventing the use of green areas for local food production to the difficulty in accessing funds, making it only possible to implement small initiatives thanks to private support.

Box 2.1. Making the food sector circular: Examples from cities

By 2050, cities will consume 80% of food. A total of 2.9 billion tonnes are destined for cities annually (resulting in 0.5 billion tonnes wasted). According to the Ellen MacArthur Foundation (2019), cities can significantly influence the way food is grown, distributed and consumed, by ensuring environmentally sustainable cultivation and by fostering the interaction with producers in their peri-urban and rural surroundings. Moreover, achieving a regenerative food system in cities will entail an annual reduction of greenhouse gas emissions by 4.3 billion tonnes of CO2 equivalent and the generation of annual benefits amounting to USD 2.7 trillion by 2050.

There are several examples of initiatives to make the food sector more circular in urban and rural areas. These initiatives focus on different aspects of the food sector dynamics, from reducing food waste (Ljubljana, Porto, Umeå), promoting urban agriculture (Brussels, Guelph, Paris), supporting local food production (Umeå), improving the co-ordination between urban and rural areas (Valladolid),

---

incorporating restaurants and the hospitality activities into these efforts (Amsterdam, Umeå, Valladolid) or the production of organic fertilisers (Porto). For example, in Spain, Valladolid's food strategy aims to improve the co-ordination across urban and rural areas and create employment opportunities whereby the city can act as an agro-incubator for responsible consumption and local production. The eco-market located in the city is the first step to providing city customers with locally grown products. The city of Toronto (Canada) put in place the "Urban Harvest" programme to help reduce food waste and benefit the broader community by collecting surplus fruits and vegetables from residents' backyards and redistributing them to local food banks and programmes. Urban Harvest also provides opportunities to learn about preserving food through canning workshops.

Source: OECD (forthcoming[9]), *The Circular Economy in Cities and Regions*, Synthesis Report, OECD Publishing, Paris; Ellen MacArthur Foundation (2019[12]), *Cities and Circular Economy for Food*, https://www.ellenmacarthurfoundation.org/assets/downloads/Cities-and-Circular-Economy-for-Food_280119.pdf (accessed on 30 April 2019).

Energy

There is an ongoing debate regarding energy transition, which can benefit the circular economy debate in Groningen. The energy sector plays an important role in production and consumption activities, in the way future infrastructure will be built and in connection with other sectors (e.g. waste). There is strong debate on the energy transition and the most suitable alternative sources of energy to respond to the demand. Hydrogen, solar energy, wind power, geothermal energy, aquathermy[4] and biogas are alternative sources of energy, shaping, amongst others, new forms of mobility and transport, agriculture and building. There is no single solution to replace the amount of energy that has been provided by natural gas during the last 60 years and that will stop after the phasing out of natural gas production established by the national authorities by 2022 (Reuters, 2019[13]).

Innovation, knowledge and capacity building play an important role in applying circular principles to the energy sector. A combination of energy alternatives is foreseen by several stakeholders and local plans. The municipality is developing "energy district plans" to provide three energy alternatives to natural gas heating in all city neighbourhoods by 2035, based on a collective heating network, electric heating and hybrid schemes combining electricity and green gas (Groningen Municipality, 2019[14]). The New Energy Coalition, created in 2017, is a network formed by business, public sector and academia representatives that is committed to promote the transition to a sustainable energy system (Energy Coalition, 2019[15]). The coalition is building knowledge on the circular economy and its relation to the energy transition, as one of the pillars of the city. It fosters innovation by connecting knowledge institutions, entrepreneurs, social organisations and governments. The Energy Transition Centre is a public-private partnership led by the Hanze University of Applied Sciences Groningen, the University of Groningen and the Energy Academy Europe that functions as a testbed for new sustainable energy technologies. Start-ups, students, scientists, businesses and public authorities share ideas and business models in an open innovation workspace collaborating to speed up the energy transition and strengthening the knowledge economy in the north of the Netherlands (EnTranCe, 2019[16]).

Building sector

The building sector has great potential to become circular. Groningen is the only city in the region where the population is projected to grow. As a consequence, during the next 20 years, a total of 20 000 new houses will be built, while those damaged by the earthquakes will have to be renovated. This is an opportunity to move from "business as usual" to a more circular approach, where materials from demolitions and secondary materials from construction can be used combined with energy and water efficiency in buildings. Newly built houses can be energy neutral as well as generating energy. Some examples of Cradle to Cradle (Box 2.2) as well as modular constructions called the New Approach (*De Nieuwe Aanpak*, DNA) can be found in Groningen (ABC2C, 2019[17]).

Box 2.2. The Cradle to Cradle approach for the building sector

Cradle to Cradle is a design concept developed in the 1990s by architect William McDonough and chemist Michael Braungart, which promotes the use of construction materials and products that are recyclable in order to respond to the challenges of waste reduction and health protection. To achieve this goal, this approach enables the design of products that can be reintroduced into new manufacturing processes after their use, adopting a different way of thinking about the design, materials and flows employed for product durability.

Since 2010, the Cradle to Cradle Products Innovation Institute manages the Cradle to Cradle Certified™ Product Standard, providing designers and manufacturers with information on product materials and manufacturing processes. It measures five key aspects: material health, material reuse, renewable energy and carbon management, water stewardship and social fairness. The product receives a grade in each category (basic, bronze, silver, gold or platinum). The product's overall qualification is equal to the lowest grade received in any of the mentioned categories. This is as a way to incentivise continuous improvements in all categories.

Some cities have already made some progress in this area:

- In 2018, the city and county of San Francisco adopted a new regulation requiring all carpet installed in city-funded construction projects to be of Cradle to Cradle Certified Product Standard. This initiative intends to address San Francisco's priorities for sustainability and material health, including the avoidance of chemicals of concern, appropriate durability, carbon impact and the use of fibre and supporting materials that contain recycled content and are themselves recyclable.
- In 2007, the city of Venlo (Netherlands) made a commitment whereby all new city buildings were to be designed by Cradle to Cradle principles and, as a result, the new city hall, built in 2016, was designed employing this method. In order to observe the benefits of the new building, measurements such as air quality and temperature were taken from the previous building and will be compared with the new one in a forthcoming comparative study. It has already been observed that the new building's facade absorbs 30% of sulphur and nitrogen oxides from the building's surroundings and in terms of economic benefits, the project is estimated to deliver a 12.5% return on investment by 2040.

Source: Cradle to Cradle Products Innovation Institute (2019[18]), *Cradle to Cradle Certified™*, http://www.c2ccertified.org/ (accessed on 30 April 2019); EPEA GmbH Website (2019[19]), *Homepage*, https://epea-hamburg.com/ (accessed on 30 April 2019); OECD (forthcoming[9]), *The Circular Economy in Cities and Regions*, Synthesis Report, OECD Publishing, Paris.

The value chain around the building sector implies a strong emphasis on design. Designers can help in the early stage of a circular economy strategy, identifying appropriate materials and making a link between demand and how people use resources. Circular building is different from sustainable building: the circular way of building consists of rethinking upstream and downstream processes to minimise waste production and maximise waste reuse. It also implies new forms of collaborations amongst designers, constructors, contractors and owners, looking at the life cycle from construction to demolition. There is a motivated community of designers in Groningen that can foster circular design. For contractors, there is a market place for reusing materials but data is lacking. The dataset Madaster aims to fill this gap, keeping track of the different material used in new and existing buildings through material passports (Box 2.3).

Box 2.3. Potential reuse of materials through material passports

Material passports are digital sets of data describing defined characteristics of materials and components in products and systems that give them value for present use, recovery and reuse. These passports are based on Cradle-to-Cradle design. They can be introduced by clients and used by architects and contractors for renovation and construction projects.

They represent a tool for improving the transparency on the materials used during construction and renovation stages. Among several benefits, they are expected to avoid costs related to the investigation of dangerous materials before demolition and enhance better asset management of constructions, since public authorities will have clearer information about materials and potential reuse.

Some stakeholders are already developing and providing these passports:

- The Dutch company Madaster is one of the companies providing digital material passports to real estate owners and property administrators.
- The company SundaHus, founded in 1990 in Sweden, provides structured material data and consulting services for sustainable development in the construction and property sectors.
- BAMB (Building As Material Banks), an EU Horizon 2020 project counting with partners from 7 European countries, has developed more than 300 digital material passports for products, materials and components.

With the objective of stimulating the reuse, the city of Amsterdam has introduced material passports as one of the main action points of its circular economy action agenda in 2016. With this in mind, one of the proposed actions consists of encouraging construction companies to use materials passports by offering discounts on plots. At a national level, the Dutch government has set up 2 investment measures to offer deductions (up to 75% of investment costs) to 310 eligible green investments, including material passports.

Source: Circle Economy/Fabric/TNO:Gemeente Amsterdam (2016[20]), *Circular Amsterdam - A Vision and Action Agenda for the City and Metropolitan Area*, https://amsterdamsmartcity.com/projects/circle-scan-amsterdam (accessed on 30 April 2019);
Luscuere, L. (2016[21]), "Materials passports: Optimising value recovery from materials", http://dx.doi.org/10.1680/jwarm.16.00016;
Madaster (2019[22]), *About Us*, https://www.madaster.com/en/about-us (accessed on 30 April 2019); Netherlands Enterprise Agency (2014[23]), *Rijksdienst voor Ondernemend Nederland*, https://www.rvo.nl/ (accessed on 11 February 2020); OECD (forthcoming[9]), *The Circular Economy in Cities and Regions*, Synthesis Report, OECD Publishing, Paris.

Urban mining can reduce raw materials extraction. Construction companies in Groningen highlight that the current regulation does not fully allow the reuse of wood. Historically, wood waste went to the landfill and nowadays is sent to incinerators. Instead, like other construction materials and under certain quality conditions, it could still be reused. As such, holding an open dialogue with companies on regulatory barriers can help find solutions. Circular Friesland, for example, is working with companies towards the constructions of the future, based on building and rebuilding energy-neutral houses and increasingly using secondary construction materials (Circulair Friesland Association, 2015[24]).

The idle capacity of buildings should also be considered for better use of resources. In the city as well as in the province, a number of disused buildings can be used as a testbed for circular economy experimentation or can have a second life, avoiding new constructions. Consumer behaviour is also changing the way spaces and buildings are used. Typically, with the increasing use of online shopping, high streets are rethinking their purpose. Empty buildings in the city centre can have an alternative use for social activities. A dataset of empty buildings can help to map these available spaces. In Groningen, a project to use the empty sugar factory aims to create a "zero-waste" neighbourhood (Box 2.4).

Box 2.4. An urban regeneration project in Groningen, Netherlands

The old sugar factory in Groningen closed down in 2010. Since then, the centrally located 120 hectares have served as an experimentation space. Until 2030, the municipality declared the area under temporary development. Nowadays over 50 initiatives (e.g. projects related to creative industries, sustainable housing programmes, music festivals and shared workspace for entrepreneurs) are being carried out in the area. By 2030, the sugar factory will become a zero-waste neighbourhood with closed material flow. It will need to generate an energetic surplus to compensate for the old buildings in the city centre that cannot be made energy neutral. The energy will be distributed through a smart grid that will ensure co-ordination between supply and demand. The planned houses in the district will include rainwater management systems to produce clean water and extract nutrients and energy from wastewater. Greywater will be purified as much as possible within the area and blackwater used for biomass and energy generation.

De Loskade, in particular, is a building project exploring the creation of a circular district within the sugar factory. The project consists of experimenting with bio-based materials and mobility, and foresees the building up of 14 houses and 32 circular apartments by 2030. *De Loskade* is projected to be a "removable" and "short stay" neighbourhood. As a "pop-up" neighbourhood, temporary properties will be dismantled once the rental period has expired in 2030 and re-built in other areas (Van Wijnen, 2019[25]). Extensive pilots and testing are taking place at *De Loskade*, with gas-free installations and off-the-grid and energy-efficient homes for example.

Source: Groningen Municipality (2019[26]), *Proposal City of Groningen for Circular and Regenerative Cties: Focus on Industrial Areas as Regenerative Drivers for the Cities of the Future*; Van Wijnen (2019[25]), *Circulariteit*, https://www.vanwijnen.nl/thema/circulariteit-2/ (accessed on 5 June 2019).

Places: Fostering urban-rural synergies for the circular economy

The metabolic connection between the city and its surroundings creates opportunities for collaboration within the circular economy approach. The traditionally close relationship between the city of Groningen and its rural surroundings has become weaker in the last decades. While the city has been increasingly conceived as a place for living and for larger industrial production, its surroundings have been strictly associated with agricultural production and the economic connection between the two has become less intense. There is a need to connect the industry sector with agriculture stakeholders and customers in urban and rural areas. Small farmers are starting to produce energy besides food, as it is more profitable due to existing incentives. Consumers are also gradually becoming potential energy producers, redefining their way of participating in the actual production processes. The local administration has a key role to facilitate a social and urban-rural dialogue in order to get them involved in the circular transition and foster new cross-cutting coalitions.

The municipality's bio-based economic vision aims to strengthen the position of Groningen as an agro-food city (Groningen Municipality, 2013[27]). Groningen presents other optimal characteristics to thrive in the bio-economy sector advancing towards circularity. First, it is located in a region with a strong agro and energy connotation. Large production of potatoes and sugar beets are also sources of secondary materials and energy, once transformed into waste. Second, it ranks high (third in the Netherlands) in the biotech sector, thanks to the presence of life science companies (EC, 2019[28]). Third, the city can further benefit from the presence of several companies which are very active in bio-economy (e.g. Attero, Avebe, Smurfit Kappa and Suiker Unie) producing energy from biomass and advancing in innovative sector research alongside the universities. In 2013, the municipality developed a bio-based strategy focusing on three strategic lines: waste collection and management; economic policy areas; and knowledge. One of the ambitions of the bio-based strategy is to reach 20% of the energy produced in the city through biomass by 2035. This will contribute to the urban energy supply planning (Groningen Municipality, 2013[27]). The presence of strong chemical, energy and agro-food sectors provide Groningen with relevant opportunities to transition to a bio-based circular economy (Groningen Municipality, 2019[29]).

Governance challenges to design and implement the circular transition

Mostly, the challenges cities and regions are facing in building circular economies are not of a technical but of an economic and governance nature. Technical solutions exist and are well known. However, to implement them, information and financial resources are needed, as well as an updated legal frameworks. Often, a holistic vision is still missing because of siloed policies. Cultural barriers are still a very important obstacle (OECD, forthcoming[9]). Key governance challenges to design and implement the circular transition in Groningen, Netherlands, are presented below.

Horizontal co-ordination (across municipal departments) can be strengthened to avoid siloed approaches while transitioning towards a circular economy. The city of Groningen has set up environmentally sustainable initiatives that can help build a narrative on the circular economy, from waste to mobility and energy. For example, initiatives include the use of hydrogen cars as sweepers and cleaners, awareness-raising and communication campaigns to reduce waste. However, these initiatives are still fragmented and would benefit from greater inter-relations with the aim of achieving common socioeconomic and environmental objectives. As such, there is room to improve effective communication in order to maximise synergies and opportunities related to the use of natural, financial and human resources. Although there are no specific joint programmes amongst municipal departments, the Department of Economics of Groningen Municipality is collaborating with the procurement, services and spatial planning, international affairs, water and waste departments for the development of a circular economy strategy.

While a number of co-ordination mechanisms exist within the regions and provinces, there is room for improvement. Partnerships and co-operation platforms across the provinces foresee joint circular economy activities. The Groningen-Assen Regional Alliance is a voluntary platform of co-operation at the scale of the functional urban area (FUA). The platform includes the provinces of Drenthe and Groningen and seven municipalities.[5] The alliance identifies construction and waste as strategic sectors to develop joint circular economy projects. The Northern Netherlands Alliance (*Samenwerkingsverband Noord-Nederland*, SNN) is a partnership amongst the three Northern provinces – Drenthe, Friesland and Groningen – and the four largest cities in the region, Assen, Emmen, Groningen and Leeuwarden. The circular economy is one of the topics incorporated into the alliance's future actions, aiming to reuse energy and waste materials at their highest quality level, while strengthening the links between natural and social capital. Different priorities can inhibit the level of effective co-ordination amongst provinces. Moreover, as highlighted above, provinces have different aims and levels of advancement towards a circular economy, the province of Friesland being the most advanced in comparison with the others. This is an advantage towards coordinated actions at territorial level, if dialogue is fostered and experiences shared.

The issue of scale is of relevance, especially for certain circular economy related activities that involve local and regional value chains. Whether the local or regional scale is appropriate depends on the type of activities, availability of resources and the existence of a market for secondary material. A local and regional economic perspective is important to strengthen the co-operation links between the city and its rural surroundings. For example, in the province of Groningen, the "Local Making Space" project (2019-20) aims to set up a local value chain and establish a link between creative industries in the city and its rural area. The initiative aims to create new products from renewable resources available within the territory of the province (House of Design, 2019[30]).

Policy coherence could be fostered to create a vision across circular economy initiatives. The circular economy approach provides an opportunity to foster complementarities across policies. Typically, synergies can be created with the City Global Climate Adaptation Centre working on agriculture and food in dry areas, sea-level rise and urban resilience. It would help the municipality to move from a reactive (e.g. focus on energy transition in reaction to the phasing out of the natural gas extractions and earthquake) to a proactive attitude, anticipating risks and creating opportunities.

Human and technical capacity should meet the needs for developing and implementing a circular economy strategy. City administrators are increasingly aware of the role of the municipality in promoting the circular economy and giving positive examples to citizens and business. As such, initiatives are in place to build capacities amongst public officers to learn about Green Public Procurement and the circular economy. Regional and local governments are in fact struggling with innovative ways of contracting. Consequently, the use of circular public procurement is still limited. This is not only due to a capacity gap but also to the difficulty in introducing clear circular related criteria for tendering. The city administration is willing to learn and build capacities for the rethinking of policies following the circular economy principles. The tender set up for the municipality's office furniture has been mentioned above as an example of a procurement procedure that incorporates circular aspects and benefits smaller firms. The tender was conferred to a regional firm that hired local companies to implement the project. Nonetheless, the municipality acknowledges that price continues to be the most decisive factor in public procurement tender selection.

In Groningen, there is room for more systematic data collection that could allow taking circular decisions, measuring progress and improving implementation. The city collects regularly data on waste collection, energy production and consumption, as well as CO2 emissions. Nonetheless, there is room for improvement in terms of data availability and frequency (e.g. regarding air pollution; waste recycling and reuse; water consumption and reuse; number of jobs per economic sector).

Funding is yet to be defined for the transition from a linear to a circular economy. As of now, provincial and regional funds directly related to the circular economy have not been allocated. On the other hand, the municipality's waste sector budget suffered cuts of more than EUR 100 million during the last 10 years due to national government decisions. Possibly, the city could benefit in the future from funds from the national government, which, in 2019, allocated an additional EUR 22.5 million in total for sustainable and circular initiatives consequent to the definition of the Circular Economy Strategy. However, it is unclear what the procedures are to access these funds and when the city of Groningen could benefit from them. The funding is linked to the envelope of EUR 300 million that the government makes available annually for the climate. In fact, the government strongly believes that the circular economy is needed to achieve climate goals and that waste is a resource. In the words of the State Secretary of Infrastructure and Water Management Stientje van Veldhoven: "Our raw materials will no longer come from an oil barrel, but from the garbage bag".[6] The EUR 22.5 million is structured as follows: EUR 10 million for stimulating reuse of plastics and consumer goods; EUR 5 million for recycling of asphalt, concrete and steel; and EUR 7.5 million have been allocated to promote climate-neutral and sustainable procurement (e.g. sustainable purchasing in the healthcare sector). Due to the lack of financial resources for innovators, only small-scale low-risk projects can actually materialise with limited impacts in terms of job creation and positive environmental effects. On the other hand, specific activities on a large scale are strongly dependent on subsidies, as in the case of green gas, which can limit the entrepreneurial initiative.

Regulatory frameworks could be adapted and updated to facilitate the transition. A range of stakeholders from waste operators to constructors in Groningen finds regulations related to waste reuse inadequate for the transition from a linear to a circular economy. There is uncertainty around the categorisation of waste streams and how materials can be reinserted in production processes when they are still reusable but by law qualified as waste. Innovative thinkers ask for a loosening up of rules (e.g. permits for waste reuse). While in some cases the local government does not have direct responsibilities to adequate the regulations to emerging needs related to the circular economy, in others some adaptation can be made (e.g. land use, permits). The legal and regulatory framework at the national level is expected to be adapted in order to make the Netherlands an economy without waste in 2050, as defined by the National Circular Economy Strategy. For example, since 2016, the national government adopted a flexible approach for amendments of the National Waste Management Plan to anticipate the changes required by the transition (Ministry of Infrastructure and the Environment/Ministry of Economic Affairs, 2016[1])). Another example is the national Smart Regulation programme (*Ruimte in Regels*) that runs up to 2020, for which the government co-operates with entrepreneurs to look for greater room for manoeuvre to promote sustainable innovations within current legislation (Ministry of Infrastructure and the Environment/Ministry of Economic Affairs, 2016[1]). In particular, in 2017, companies in the wind energy sector contacted the Smart Regulation programme's helpdesk specialised in the chemistry sector to raise the issue of the restrictive regulations regarding the inability to reuse plastic turbine blades for windmills after their replacement. This plastic is now used as an input in the car and ship industry (Ministry of Economic Affairs, 2017[31]).

While technical solutions are available, there is room for developing non-technical innovation in the circular economy. Pilot initiatives aim to: make the chemical and plastics industry more sustainable, replacing fossil fuels with bio-products (Bio BTX); develop innovative research for the reuse of organic potato waste and the production of plant-based protein (Avebe); generate bioplastics from biomass (Suiker Unie); and provide district heating using green gas (Bareau). Regardless of how successful the pilot initiatives are, they intend to provide new techniques that can be used to concretise circular processes. However, beyond technical innovations, non-technical ones should be set in terms of collaboration and public procurement. For example, the *De Loskade* circular district experimentation (see Box 2.4) could inform, through the results of the innovations (in this case a potential city district), future city urban plans (e.g. including housing, land use and mobility) and selection criteria for innovative public tenders concerning buildings and infrastructure. Three types of challenges still remain: i) to increase the acceptance of circular models by users of services and products; ii) to clearly understand costs and benefits to help entrepreneurs shift from linear to circular production models- at present, embracing circular principles is very much related to the willingness of innovative thinkers and forward-looking, less risk-averse entrepreneurs-; iii) to scale up the projects once they pass the pilot phase.

Even though there is a high level of participation from various stakeholders in policymaking and implementation in the city of Groningen, stakeholder engagement can in some cases be challenging. Stakeholder engagement requires active, specific and tailored communication strategies. The main issue is to involve a great number of people and not only the "happy few". Circular entrepreneurs in Groningen find it difficult to get people involved in even the smallest of activities (e.g. urban gardening), aiming to raise awareness and stimulate more sustainable behaviour concerning the use (and reuse) of resources. Changing "business as usual" and contributing to a behavioural shift is not an easy task, especially when risks, costs and benefits are unclear.

References

ABC2C (2019), *Homepage*, https://abc2c.nl/over-abc2c/ (accessed on 26 July 2019). [17]

Circle Economy/Fabric/TNO:Gemeente Amsterdam (2016), *Circular Amsterdam - A Vision and Action Agenda for the City and Metropolitan Area*, https://amsterdamsmartcity.com/projects/circle-scan-amsterdam (accessed on 30 April 2019). [20]

Circulair Friesland Association (2015), *Circulair Fryslân*, https://www.urgenda.nl/documents/CirculairFryslan2.pdf (accessed on 2 May 2019). [24]

CO_2 Monitor Groningen (2018), *CO_2-Monitor Groningen*, https://www.groningenco2neutraal.nl/ (accessed on 29 April 2019). [11]

Cradle to Cradle Products Innovation Institute (2019), *Cradle to Cradle Certified™*, http://www.c2ccertified.org/ (accessed on 30 April 2019). [18]

EC (2019), *Province of Groningen - Internal Market, Industry, Entrepreneurship and SMEs*, European Commision, https://ec.europa.eu/growth/tools-databases/regional-innovation-monitor/base-profile/province-groningen (accessed on 22 July 2019). [3]

EC (2019), *Province of Groningen - Internal Market, Industry, Entrepreneurship and SMEs*, European Commission, https://ec.europa.eu/growth/tools-databases/regional-innovation-monitor/base-profile/province-groningen (accessed on 29 April 2019). [28]

Ellen MacArthur Foundation (2019), *Cities and Circular Economy for Food*, https://www.ellenmacarthurfoundation.org/assets/downloads/Cities-and-Circular-Economy-for-Food_280119.pdf (accessed on 30 April 2019). [12]

Energy Coalition (2019), *New Energy Coalition: we know energy transition*. [15]

EnTranCe (2019), *About EnTranCe*, https://www.en-tran-ce.org/en/over-entrance/ (accessed on 29 April 2019). [16]

EPEA GmbH (2019), *Homepage*, https://epea-hamburg.com/ (accessed on 30 April 2019). [19]

EU Eden Project (2002), *Waste Neutral - A Sustainable Approach to Waste and Resource Management*, Eden Project, http://ec.europa.eu/environment/archives/waste/pdf_comments/eden_annex.pdf (accessed on 6 June 2019). [32]

Groningen Municipality (2019), *Chemistry*, Groningen.nl, https://groningen.nl/en/do-business/sector-information/chemistry (accessed on 29 April 2019). [29]

Groningen Municipality (2019), *Introduction to Groningen - The Circular Innovation Hub*. [7]

Groningen Municipality (2019), *Neighborhood Energy Plans*, https://gemeente.groningen.nl/wijkenergieplannen (accessed on 22 November 2019). [14]

Groningen Municipality (2019), *Proposal City of Groningen for Circular and Regenerative Cties: Focus on Industrial Areas as Regenerative Drivers for the Cities of the Future*. [26]

Groningen Municipality (2018), *Council Proposal: Groningen Circular*. [5]

Groningen Municipality (2013), *Op weg naar een groene kringloop-economie*, [27]
https://gemeente.groningen.nl/sites/default/files/groningen-visie-biobasedeconomy.pdf
(accessed on 29 April 2019).

House of Design (2019), *Homepage*, http://www.houseofdesign.nl/en/ (accessed on [30]
26 July 2019).

Koploperproject (2019), *Front Runner Project (Koploperproject)*, https://www.koploperproject- [8]
groningen.nl/zo-werkt-het (accessed on 26 November 2019).

Luscuere, L. (2016), "Materials passports: Optimising value recovery from materials", [21]
http://dx.doi.org/10.1680/jwarm.16.00016.

Madaster (2019), *About Us*, https://www.madaster.com/en/about-us (accessed on [22]
30 April 2019).

Metabolic (2018), "Metabolic pioneers urban and regional approaches for Circular Economy", [4]
https://www.metabolic.nl/news/metabolic-pioneers-urban-and-regional-approaches-for-
circular-economy/ (accessed on 30 April 2019).

Ministry of Economic Affairs (2017), *Better Regulation: Towards a Responsible Reduction in the* [31]
Regulatory Burden 2012-2017,
https://www.government.nl/documents/reports/2017/08/22/better-regulation-towards-a-
responsible-reduction-in-the-regulatory-burden-2012-2017 (accessed on 27 November 2019).

Ministry of Infrastructure and the Environment/Ministry of Economic Affairs (2016), *A Circular* [1]
Economy in the Netherlands by 2050, https://www.government.nl/topics/circular-
economy/accelerating-the-transition-to-a-circular-economy (accessed on 27 November 2019).

Netherlands Enterprise Agency (2019), *Rijksdienst voor Ondernemend Nederland*, [2]
https://www.rvo.nl/ (accessed on 11 February 2020).

Netherlands Entreprise Agency (2014), *Tax Relief Schemes for Environmentally Friendly* [23]
Investment (Vamil and MIA), http://www.rvo.nl (accessed on 29 April 2019).

Nord Regio (2018), *Developing and Managing Innovation Ecosystems in the Circular Economy*, [33]
http://norden.diva-portal.org/smash/get/diva2:1240777/FULLTEXT01.pdf (accessed on
6 June 2019).

OECD (2019), *OECD Survey on the Circular Economy in Cities and Regions*, OECD, Paris. [6]

OECD (2016), *Water Governance in Cities*, https://www.oecd-ilibrary.org/governance/water- [10]
governance-in-cities_9789264251090-en (accessed on 6 February 2020).

OECD (forthcoming), *The Circular Economy in Cities and Regions*, Synthesis Report, OECD [9]
Publishing, Paris.

Reuters (2019), "Netherlands to halt Groningen gas production by 2022 - Reuters", [13]
https://www.reuters.com/article/us-netherlands-gas/netherlands-to-halt-groningen-gas-
production-by-2022-idUSKCN1VV1KE (accessed on 26 November 2019).

Van Wijnen (2019), *Circulariteit*, https://www.vanwijnen.nl/thema/circulariteit-2/ (accessed on [25]
5 June 2019).

Notes

[1] Waste neutrality at the city level aims to achieve, within the different waste streams, a volume of recyclables leaving the city that is equal or smaller than the volume of products made from recyclables that enter the city (EU Eden Project, 2002[32]).

[2] Ecosystems promotes regional economic growth through close collaboration between members (e.g. companies, research institutes and public authorities) (Nord Regio, 2018[33]).

[1] The plant has a separation capacity of 810 000 tonnes/3 lines and an incineration capacity of 625 000 tonnes/3 furnaces.

[2] A project co-funded by the North Sea Region Programme 2014-20 and involving five different countries in the North Sea Region (Belgium, Denmark, Germany, the Netherlands and Sweden).

[3] It brings together 450 rural entrepreneurs, industry and logistical companies and governments.

[4] Thermal energy form wastewater and surface water.

[5] These are Assen, Groningen, Het Hogeland, Midden Groningen, Noordenveld, Tynaarlo and Westerkwartier

[6] https://www.rijksoverheid.nl/actueel/nieuws/2018/10/10/klimaatenvelop-225-miljoen-voor-circulaire-economie.

3 Policy recommendations and actions for a circular economy in Groningen, Netherlands

In response to the challenges identified in Chapter 2, this chapter suggests some policy recommendations to implement a circular economy in the city of Groningen, Netherlands. The policy recommendations are accompanied by a list of actions for concrete implementation, according to international practices.

Introduction

A total of 17 recommendations have been identified accordingly to the role of the city as promoter, facilitator and enabler of the circular economy (Table 3.1). These recommendations are accompanied by a set of actions aiming to support Groningen's transition to a circular economy. The proposed actions are indicative and based on international practices while taking into account the local context. These international practices carried out in the field of the circular economy by cities, regions and national governments can serve as inspiration for the implementation of the recommendations. As such, they are not expected to be replicated in Groningen but rather provide the municipality with a set of examples for the development and implementation of the suggested actions.

Table 3.1. Policy recommendations for the circular economy in Groningen, Netherlands

Promoter	Facilitator	Enabler
Make the city a role model	Facilitate co-ordination across municipal departments and across regional and provincial governments	Identify the regulatory instruments that need to be adapted to foster the transition to a circular economy
Develop a circular economy strategy	Facilitate practice exchange amongst public, not-for-profit actors and businesses	Identify financial and economic conditions and opportunities for circular economy initiatives
Promote a circular economy culture	Facilitate the connection between businesses and universities	Implement Green Public Procurement
Promote labels and certifications	Establish a single window for circular businesses and support entrepreneurship	Develop training programmes on the circular economy
Create demand by being a launching customer	Strengthen the existing networks to pick the "low-hanging fruits" from co-operation of local businesses	Create spaces for experimentation
	Facilitate the connection between urban and rural areas	Develop an information, monitoring and evaluation system

It is important to note that:

- **Actions are neither compulsory nor binding**: Identified actions address a variety of ways to implement and achieve objectives. However, they are neither compulsory nor binding. They represent suggestions, for which adequacy and feasibility should be carefully evaluated by the municipality of Groningen in an inclusive manner, involving stakeholders as appropriate. In turn, the combination of more than one action can be explored, if necessary.

- **Prioritisation of actions should be considered**: Taking into account the unfeasibility of addressing all recommendations at the same time, prioritisation is key. As such, steps taken towards a circular transition should be progressive.

- **Resources for implementation should be assessed**: The implementation of actions will require human, technical and financial resources. When prioritising and assessing the adequacy and feasibility of the suggested actions, the resources needed to put them in practice should be carefully evaluated, as well as the role of stakeholders that can contribute to the implementation phase.

- **The proposed actions should be updated in the future**: New potential steps and objectives may emerge as actions start to be implemented.

- **Several stakeholders should contribute to their implementation:** Policy recommendations and related actions should be implemented as a shared responsibility across a wide range of actors. The stakeholder groups contributing to this report and to the identification of the actions are represented in Figure 3.1. They have a key role as "do-ers" of the circular economy system in Groningen, Netherlands, along with other stakeholders that will be engaged in the future.

Figure 3.1. Stakeholders map in Groningen, Netherlands

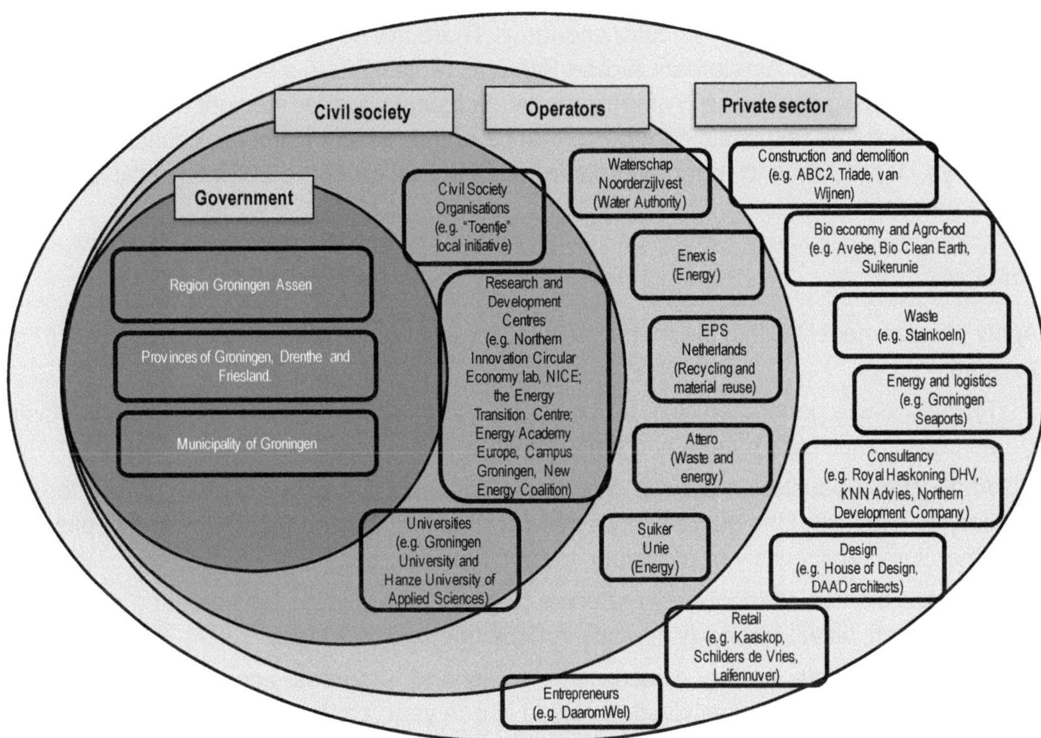

Note: This stakeholders map is based on the 30+ stakeholders that took part in 2 OECD missions to the city of Groningen, Netherlands, in February and September 2019.

The city of Groningen can play a role as promoter, facilitator and enabler of the circular economy strategy. Cities act as *promoters* when they identify priorities, promote concrete projects and engage stakeholders; they are *facilitators* when fostering co-operation between stakeholders, citizens and levels of government. The city's *enabler* role entails setting the necessary conditions for the circular economy (e.g. updating regulatory frameworks, catalysing funds, etc.). In order to boost the circular economy in Groningen, the municipality could implement the recommendations detailed in this section.

Promoting a vision and a strategy for the circular economy

The city of Groningen can play an important role in promoting the circular economy in the city and its surrounding area. It is widely recognised that Groningen, being the biggest city and the only one expecting population growth in the Northern Netherlands region, can play a lead role in the transition from a linear to a circular economy. It is also important for the city to give a positive example to businesses and citizens for the circular economy to happen and to promote behavioural change. The following section presents possible actions Groningen could implement to boost the circular economy.

Make the city a role model

Making the city a role model for the circular economy would trigger behavioural and business change inside and outside the city. The recipe of success consists in taking risks and accepting failures. The municipality should be an example of change and make this an explicit target, while showing the feasibility of the circular transition with concrete actions. The local government should take the initiative of using sustainable products and building infrastructure in a circular manner, e.g. from roads to buildings. This would send a positive signal to the market and would help brand the city with a new image for the whole country, moving out from a natural gas extraction to a circular economy. There are several examples of cities going in this direction and specific actions: Amsterdam Airport Schiphol rents light as a service instead adhering to the traditional model of buying light bulbs. With this model, Schiphol pays for the light it uses while Philips, as owner of all installations, is responsible for performance and durability (Circular Economy Club, 2019[1]) . The city of Tokyo, Japan, aims to rent materials for the celebration of the 2020 Olympic Games, leasing them after the games.

Key actions:

- Apply circular models within the municipality according to the "practice what you preach" principle, such as:
  - o Reduce waste generation (e.g. reducing the use of paper or banning single-use plastics such as cups in municipal events and daily activities).
  - o Apply the product-as-a-service model through public procurement (e.g. pay for a lighting service adapted to the municipality's needs rather than buying light bulbs and appliances; lease a furniture service instead of buying specific furniture, etc.).
  - o Promote the use of secondary materials (e.g. all public plastic bins must be made of recycled plastics, an initiative already in place in Groningen since 2018).
- Clearly communicate to the citizens the goals and progress achieved by the municipality (e.g. percentage of single-use plastic avoided in one year, etc.).

Develop a circular economy strategy

Developing a circular economy strategy would help define priorities and allocate funds. The strategy would serve to build a strong and global vision and a relevant narrative of the circular economy in Groningen that could ensure co-operation across actors and long-term political buy-in. The strategy would enable the circular economy transition beyond electoral cycles, identifying short-, medium- and long-term goals and actions, with the help of stakeholders, to which the municipality is accountable. Furthermore, it would enhance coherence across existing initiatives, develop deeper knowledge of existing material flows in the city, promote better use of resources and more efficient logistics. Examples of circular economy strategies in cities and regions are presented in Table 3.2.

Table 3.2. Circular economy initiatives at the subnational level

City	Country	Initiative
Amsterdam	Netherlands	"Amsterdam Circular 2020-25" (2019)
Barcelona Metropolitan Area (AMB)	Spain	Circular economy promotion programme AMB circular (2019): i) Industrial Symbiosis Metropolitan Project ii) Platform of Natural Resources iii) Circular Economy Table
Brussels Capital Region	Belgium	Regional Programme for the Circular Economy 2016-20 (PREC)
Flanders	Belgium	Circular Flanders, 2016
Nantes	France	Circular Economy Roadmap Nantes (2018) (*Feuille de route économie circulaire Nantes Métropole*)
Paris	France	Circular Economy Plan 2017-20 (2017) (*Plan économie circulaire de Paris 2017-20*)

City	Country	Initiative
Rotterdam	Netherlands	Rotterdam Circularity Programme 2019-23
Scotland	United Kingdom	"Making Things Last: A Circular Economy Strategy for Scotland" (2016)
Tilburg	Netherlands	Tilburg Circular Agenda 2019
Valladolid	Spain	Valladolid Circular Economy Roadmap (2017-18)

Source: OECD (forthcoming[2]), *The Circular Economy in Cities and Regions*, Synthesis Report, OECD Publishing, Paris.

Key actions:

Urban metabolism analysis

- Collaborate with universities to carry out an urban metabolism study for Groningen.
- Evaluate the scale of the analysis at the metropolitan and regional levels, with the collaboration of competent authorities.
- Disseminate the results of the metabolism analysis and clearly communicate them to the public.
- Repeat the metabolism flow analysis after a certain period of time (e.g. a year).

Map existing circular initiatives in various sectors

This will enable the city to frame priorities and actions in the short, medium and long term, as well as identify circular sectors and synergies across them. It would also help to improve existing policies and explore the main gaps. Steps are:

- Collect information on existing "circular economy-related initiatives", such as projects, programmes and plans in various sectors (e.g. food, waste, water, transport, etc.), which implement for example:
  - Regenerative design.
  - Sustainable production practices based on reducing virgin material extraction.
  - Last-mile distribution practices.
  - Sustainable consumption patterns aiming at reducing waste.
- Explore different ways to conduct the mapping, for example through:
  - An online platform to upload initiatives and register projects in the field of the circular economy. It could take the form of an open-source database to be able to research any aspect of circular initiatives. A communication campaign to reach out to all stakeholders will be needed.
  - Offline platforms, gathering input from stakeholders through regular meetings, surveys, interviews and public consultations.
- Identify the core motivations and benefits of the businesses undertaking these initiatives. Consider the following options:
  - Surveys.
  - Meetings/interviews.
  - Public consultations.
  - Events/seminars.
- Update and share the information collected through the mapping.

Define goals and actions

- Define result-oriented and realistic objectives, and ensure that they are coherent with the national and regional levels.

- Define short-, medium- and long-term targets and sub-targets for the circular strategy (e.g. quantity of circular economy-related projects, number of circular building to be constructed, etc.).

Engage stakeholders

The circular economy is a shared responsibility across stakeholders that need to be involved from the phase zero of the strategy to build consensus and vision. The implementation of the circular economy strategy is not just the responsibility of the municipality. Innovative thinkers and motivated entrepreneurs can be consulted to start pioneering activities for example in the agro-food and bio-economy sectors. Architects, urban planners and representatives from the creative industry sector can help with eco-design and in the construction and demolition fields, etc. Steps consist of (OECD, 2015[3]):

- Designing a participative methodology to engage key stakeholders to work on the definition and co-creation of a shared circular economy strategy that reflects their concerns:
  - Map all stakeholders that have a stake in the outcome or are likely to be affected, as well as their responsibility, core motivations and interactions.
  - Define the ultimate line of decision-making, the objectives of stakeholder engagement and the expected use of input.
  - Use stakeholder engagement techniques, ensuring the effective representation of all stakeholders in the process.
  - Allocate proper financial and human resources and share needed information for result-oriented stakeholder engagement.
  - Regularly assess the process and outcomes of stakeholder engagement to learn, adjust and improve accordingly.
  - Embed engagement processes in clear legal and policy frameworks, organisational structures/principles and responsible authorities.
  - Customise the type and level of engagement to the needs and keeping the process flexible to changing circumstances.
  - Clarify how the inputs will be used.
- Organising communication campaigns and activities in the city to raise awareness among stakeholders on the circular economy's objectives and benefits and how citizens can contribute.
- Creating participation spaces for citizens and stakeholders throughout the different implementation phases of the circular economy strategy. Instruments that can be used to share the ownership of the circular economy transition with stakeholders include:
  - Multi-stakeholder fora.
  - Workshops.
  - Breakfast meetings on the circular economy.
  - Co-creation methodologies.
  - Feedback loops.

Identify links and synergies

- With existing strategies on climate change, waste and urban plans.
- With the digital sector (e.g. cyber safety, big data and blockchain, and 5G rollout).

Develop a financial plan

- Design a set of actions to put in place the defined objectives, set their expected outcomes and allocate a budget and resources (human and technical) to each of the actions.

- Develop a financial plan for the implementation of the strategy and include it as a part of the implementation process.
- Take into account alternative funding options from all levels of government (e.g. funding to promote the circular economy from the Dutch national Ministry of Infrastructure, the national regional strategies and the SDG implementation programme.

Monitoring, evaluation and communication

- Regularly monitor the progress of the strategy's implementation; evaluate its impacts to make improvements and communicate the results to the public.
- Explore the available indicators and measurable targets (economic, social and environmental) that can be useful for monitoring the strategy. The indicators proposed by the OECD (forthcoming[2]) can be taken into account:

Setting the strategy

- No. of public administrations/departments involved in the design of the circular economy imitative.
- No. of actions identified to achieve the objectives.
- No. of circular economy projects to implement the actions.
- No. of staff employed for the circular economy initiative's design within the city/region/administration.
- No. of stakeholders involved to co-create the circular economy imitative.
- No. of projects financed by the city/regional government/Total number of projects.
- No. of projects financed by the private sectors/Total number of projects.

Implementing the strategy

- Waste diverted from landfill (T/inhabitant/year or %).
- CO_2 emission avoided (T CO_2/capita or %).
- Raw material avoided (T/inhabitant/year or %).
- Use of recovered material (T/inhabitant/year or %).
- Energy savings (Kgoe/inhabitant/year or %).
- Water savings (ML/inhabitant/year or %).
- Clearly communicate the aim and the expected outputs of the strategy.

Promote a circular economy culture

Raise awareness of the circular economy among citizens, businesses and relevant actors and encourage sustainable production and consumption practices would promote a circular economy culture. This can be done through furthering communication (through a dedicated website, communication campaigns, sharing success stories in the media to promote projects and initiatives) and creating spaces for meetings and dialogues. For example, the city of Valladolid (Spain) organises Circular Weekends, during which entrepreneurs connect with one another and join forces on circular projects. Another way to strengthen the circular community would be through "circular economy ambassadors". The London Waste and Recycling Board (United Kingdom) has started recruiting "circular economy ambassadors" in different companies and local authorities to share the benefits of the circular economy with specific information for each economic sector and to raise awareness in the workplace (LWARB, 2017[4]). In North Karelia (Finland), a regional co-ordination group organises seminars on different topics related to the circular economy in order to raise awareness (OECD, forthcoming[2]).

Key actions:

- Create a dedicated website in order to share knowledge and good practices concerning the circular economy.
- Launch communication campaigns based on success stories and communicate on how citizens and different actors can contribute to it.
- Organise events for knowledge sharing, networking and the promotion of the circular economy at the local level.
- Use social media for quick updates dedicated to circular economy initiatives.
- Promote the creation of a group of businesses focused on the circular economy.
- Promote communications and events for children and students.

Promote labels and certifications

Promoting competition of ideas, awards and certifications for circular economy initiatives would stimulate new ideas and projects and provide implementation support, including funding opportunities and spaces for experimentation. For example, the *White Paper on the Circular Economy of Greater Paris (France)* includes a proposal to design and use circular economy labels (City of Paris, 2015[5]).

Key actions:

- Consider developing a local label or certification for products, initiatives or organisations that are implementing circular practices in Groningen (e.g. certifications asserting that products manufactured at a local level are produced using secondary materials, etc.).
- Collaborate with universities and research centres to analyse the criteria for circular certifications/labels. For example:
  - Use of recycled materials.
  - Life-cycle analysis.
  - Present a plan for disposal of materials or parts.
  - Extended product lifespan (e.g. long guarantee, reuse of spare parts of a product).
  - Product-as-a-service concept.
- Undertake pilot experiments on circular certificates/labelling.
- Engage in a dialogue with the private sector in order to discuss the development of a local declaration for businesses and organisations to express their commitment with the circular transition.
- Define common guidelines for circular economy products and processes at a local level.
- Promote systematic recognition of good circular practices.

Create demand by being a launching customer

The city can be the first customer to stimulate demand and help business small- and medium-sized enterprises (SMEs), entrepreneurs and start-ups. More specifically, circular design products and technological solutions (e.g. in the recycling processes) need demand for them to be in the market. The local government can stimulate this demand by being the first customer of innovative products and goods. For example, Start-up in Residence (San Francisco, United States) and the Amsterdam Circular Challenge (Amsterdam, Netherlands) connect start-ups and businesses to provide solutions to the city's problems through transparent selection processes. If the solution provided by a project proves successful, the municipality invests in it or becomes its launching customer. A similar scheme has been adopted by the

Dutch national government: through the "Circular Challenge Project", the government supports financially profitable business cases and can act as a "launching customer" (Ministry of Infrastructure and the Environment/Ministry of Economic Affairs, 2016[6]).

Key actions:

- Define the key challenges that the city would like to address through the possible solutions provided by entrepreneurs, start-ups or companies.
  - o Define themes (e.g. related to waste, safety, health, tourism, mobility, technology, etc.).
  - o Define steps, procedures and clear rules.
  - o Set targets to be reached through the activities.
  - o Measure impacts and provide concrete figures.
- Organise a call for projects.
- Allocate the necessary human and financial resources for evaluating and monitoring the selected initiatives.

Facilitating multilevel co-ordination for the circular economy

The municipality can facilitate collaborations and co-operation among a wide range of actors to make the circular economy happen on the ground. The following section presents potential actions.

Facilitate co-ordination across municipal departments and across regional and provincial governments

Co-ordination across municipal department has several objectives, such as: strengthening synergies across municipal departments to avoid duplications, overlaps and grey areas; clarifying the targets and expectations of the circular economy initiatives within the municipality; developing a common narrative throughout municipal departments while aligning targets. Since circular economy-related activities go beyond the city's burdens (e.g. input and output of energy, resources and material concern the entire region), it is important to create spaces for dialogue and experience exchange, enhancing common actions and learning processes. Co-ordination across levels of government could: address common circular economy-related issues; align objectives between the city and the region that may hamper the achievement of long-term targets; avoid asymmetries or lack of information between the actors at the local and regional levels. There are several international experiences: to foster co-ordination across municipal departments (horizontal), the cities of Melbourne (Australia), Toronto (Canada) and Oulu (Finland) have created dedicated horizontal working groups, while the Metropolitan Area of Barcelona has formed a body for the co-ordination of Barcelona and neighbouring municipalities within the metropolitan area (OECD, forthcoming[2]). Examples of co-ordination across levels of government (vertical) include: the Spanish national strategy creating an inter-ministerial body bringing together the national government, the autonomous regions and the local governments in the Spanish Federation of Municipalities and Provinces (FEMP); and the Brussels region (Belgium) regional programme for the circular economy (2016-20) co-ordinated by three ministries and four regional administrative bodies.

Key actions:

Co-ordination across municipal departments

- Identify how municipal departments can relate to the circular economy in their policies (e.g. public procurement, environment, innovation, etc.).

- Consider appointing a person or a team responsible for co-ordinating the circular economy strategy with a clear mandate.
- Define the co-ordination tools:
  o Ad hoc meetings.
  o Permanent working group on the circular economy.
  o Technical and political board.
  o Inter-departmental programmes.
  o Co-ordination group of experts.

Co-ordination across levels of government

- Set up a co-ordination platform across the municipality, provinces and region for co-operation on circular economy-related policies. The following governance instruments could be considered:
  o Bodies between regional and local authorities can take the form of committees, commissions, agencies or working groups.
  o Ad hoc meetings for city-province-region co-ordination.
  o Co-operation agreements between Groningen, the region, the three provinces and other municipalities in the region for the implementation of joint projects on the circular economy.
  o Joint actions between the municipality and the region, and set up of pilot projects.
  o Roadmap developed together with the region for co-ordination, harmonisation of objectives and implementation.
  o Shared databases and information systems.

Facilitate practice exchange amongst public, not-for-profit actors and businesses

Facilitating practice exchange amongst public, not-for-profit actors and businesses may foster business opportunities and innovation. For example, a dedicated webpage containing information on circular economy-related activities, sectors and stakeholders can represent the basis for possible new collaborations, while raising awareness of existing opportunities. Several cities and regions have developed online platforms to provide: an online portal on the circular economy (Paris, France), waste-related information in real time (North Karelia, Finland) or open data (Toronto, United States). The city of Austin (United States) created a materials marketplace to foster secondary materials exchanges; Phoenix (United States) developed an online zero-waste assistant to provide recycling information to local residents.

Key actions:

- Create a dedicated webpage containing information on circular economy-related activities, stakeholders involved and calls for projects.
- Create an online or offline platform/network to share good practices and challenges for SMEs and entrepreneurs on the transition to a circular economy.
- Monitor development and activities on the online information platform (e.g. number of updates, their frequency, information uses, etc.).

Facilitate the connection between businesses and universities

Facilitating the connection between businesses and universities stimulates innovation. The municipality can be the link between universities, expecting to develop further knowledge on circular dimensions (e.g. in bio-economy and circular design) and the business sector, looking for new specialised employees in specific sectors. The city could develop an "ecosystem" for the circular economy, fostering collaboration amongst universities, businesses and the government, following existing experiences on digital society and healthy ageing (triple-helix collaboration). The municipality can also create the conditions for start-ups to focus on circular economy-related activities, according to the needs expressed by the municipality itself and in collaboration with research centres and labs. It could provide start-ups and scale-ups with access to business partners, ideas, clients, financing and help share knowledge and expertise, build knowledge for a broad understanding of the circular economy and promote pioneering activities and business models. Together with Arizona State University, the city of Phoenix (United States) created a Resource Innovation and Solutions Network (RISN) Incubator for accompanying businesses in the shift towards a circular economy.

Key actions:

- Consider financial instruments to link the private sector with universities. Some examples are:
  - Research and development (R&D) and innovation subsidies.
  - Financial support to create academic spin-offs and for firms to purchase R&D services from certified researchers from universities.
  - Tax breaks and social security exemptions to companies that hire recent master's/PhD graduates on circular economy areas.
- Explore potential collaborations across business and universities to strengthen the link between the digital sector in the city and the circular economy (e.g. cyber safety, big data, blockchain, and the 5G rollout). Examples applying digital technologies to the circular economy are:
  - Smart sensors to track and monitor material and resource flows in the city (e.g. waste collection data).
  - Digital material passports and digital material exchange platforms in the construction sector, to make materials information clear and accessible, via open-source software. Box 2.3 presents international examples of material passport platforms.

Establish a single window for circular businesses and support entrepreneurship

Establishing a single window for circular businesses and entrepreneurship could aim to offer all services, information and administrative support regarding circular economy projects for businesses, in order to reduce transaction costs for entrepreneurs and SMEs willing to be part of the transition. Although not strictly related to the circular economy, the following experiences could provide examples for potential procedures that could be adapted to the design and implementation of circular economy initiatives. In Romania, the National Trade Register Office (Ministry of Justice) operates a single-window shop (*Biroul Unic*) for business registration in a period of three days. Hungary has established a central electronic contact point to facilitate starting a business or providing services in Hungary (OECD, 2010[7]). The initiative Start-up Slovenia, established in 2014, aims to raise the level of entrepreneurial talent by developing networks that encourage company growth on international markets, contribute to higher capital accessibility and activate various ecosystem stakeholders. The initiative mobilises a network of mentors from various backgrounds to provide entrepreneurs and young firms with tailored advice (OECD, 2019[8]).

Key actions:

- Define a set of circular services, information and support offered by the single window for circular businesses.
- Clarify the objective of the single window for circular businesses (e.g. offer all services, information and administrative support regarding circular economy projects for businesses).

- Provide information on registration, legal framework and investment climate.
- Provide services to speed up the granting of necessary permits and licenses in a centralised and comprehensive manner.
- Provide specific assistance with registration procedures.
- Support entrepreneurship through tax exemption, when possible, capacity building programmes and clear information.
- Launch incubators to foster knowledge sharing and pilot testing.

Strengthen the existing networks to pick the "low-hanging fruits" from co-operation of local businesses

Strengthening the existing networks to pick the "low-hanging fruits" from co-operation of local businesses could make them an active part of the circular economy transition. The networks (e.g. the Food Network, BUILT-IN Groningen) could include additional actors, generating activities related to the reuse of materials, engagement of local communities, etc. with the support of the municipality, when possible (e.g. space, funds, awareness-raising). In 2018, the city of Amsterdam launched the Circular Hotels Leaders Group (*Kloplopergroep*). A total of 12 hotels have started co-operating amongst themselves and with actors along their different value chains (e.g. by exchanging knowledge; joint purchasing and bundling of waste streams). In Umeå (Sweden), through the Sustainable Restaurants Network (*Hållbara Restauranger*), the municipality helps restaurants become more sustainable and, in the long run, makes it easier for Umeå's residents to consume sustainably when eating out. In 2017, the network started with four restaurants but today involves ten additional ones. The network is also developing a certification to show customers which restaurants are incorporating more sustainable ways of working.

Key actions:

- Identify existing networks, their mission and the link to the circular economy (how they can contribute to the transition).
- Determine local networks' needs (e.g. space to develop activities, access to funds or raising awareness).
- Provide support to existing networks. Possible instruments could be:
  - Space for experimentation.
  - Networking and platform events.
  - Online platforms for information sharing.

Facilitate the connection between urban and rural areas

The local administration has a key role in facilitating a social and urban-rural dialogue in order to get farmers, SMEs, consumers, businesses and knowledge institutions involved in the circular transition and foster new cross-cutting solutions (e.g. some key sectors are bio-economy, food, biomass, construction, delivery, farming, agriculture, chemistry). This would help foster a territorial approach of the circular economy, integrating rural areas as part of the solution, encouraging regional changes in production and consumption practices, and promoting co-operation experiences between SMEs, consumers and knowledge institutions. There are international experiences advancing towards improving urban-rural connections towards a circular economy. Kitakyushu City (Japan) has established a food-recycling loop between rural-urban areas, while in Tampere (Finland), eco-fellows are co-ordinating rural-urban partnerships related to biogas: they work as a hub that brings together different actors not used to being in contact (farms, power plant operators, logistics, etc.). Since 2016, Start-up Sweden, a boot camp for digital start-ups from rural areas in Sweden, is connecting start-ups from rural areas across the country with the entrepreneurial ecosystem in Stockholm. The boot camp takes place four times a year, with each boot camp providing ten companies with the opportunity to go to Stockholm and expand their networks via contacts with other companies, investors, potential customers and partners (OECD, 2019[8]).

Key actions:

- Establish rural-urban partnerships for creating products, material and service loops (OECD, 2013[9]).
- Create circular loops in the agro-food and bio-economy sector; use of organic waste as fertiliser; last-mile type of food production and distribution, etc.
- Foster collaboration across agro-businesses located in the rural area of the city with universities and research centres. For example: to reduce packaging, use of plastic, use various type of waste as resource; reduce transport form the urban centre to the surrounding area and vice versa.

Enabling the economics and governance conditions for the uptake of the circular economy

Implementing a circular economy entails enabling the necessary governance and economic conditions. As such, the city government could explore the following policy alternatives.

Identify the regulatory instruments that need to be adapted to foster the transition to a circular economy

Clarifying the regulatory framework for circular economy practices and addressing overlaps and gaps in regulatory functions would imply a dialogue with the national, regional governments when responsibility goes beyond that of the municipality. Also, it would be key to identify cases in which regulations (e.g. land use, permits) can be adapted at the local level. The city of Amsterdam (Netherlands) developed tenders for land allocation, primarily for new-build projects (*Roadmap Circular Land Tendering* (City of Amsterdam, 2019[10])) and supported the creation of a circular neighbourhood, Circular Buiksloterham. Once one of the most polluted areas in the city, it is now turning into a circular area for living and working. The type of innovations and solutions promoted by these experiences in terms of urban planning and land tendering (e.g. circular construction, changing of land use) helped overcome the actual administrative, legal and financial obstacles that they face (City of Amsterdam, 2019[10]). In Spain, in 2013, the city of Barcelona launched the pilot programme called Superblocks to respond to the scarcity of green spaces, the high levels of pollution, the high rate of environmental noise, accident data and sedentary lifestyle. Superblocks are urban cells of about 400 m2 that allow vehicles to circulate only along the perimeter roads, while interior streets are reserved for pedestrians and, under special conditions, certain types of traffic (e.g. resident vehicles, services, emergencies, loading and unloading activities). To do this, land-use regulations and mobility plans have been adapted with the aim of reclaiming public space for citizens, making the city more liveable and reducing pollution and carbon emissions.

Key actions:

- Organise ad hoc meetings or public consultations to build a dialogue across the city council, civil society and private sector to identify the main regulatory and legal barriers and sectors in which actions can be taken (e.g. energy system, second-hand materials, the digital sector, etc.).
- Establish a dialogue with the national and regional governments to identify regulatory instruments that can encourage the transition towards a circular economy, as well as gaps (in particular, when the regulatory and fiscal responsibilities go beyond that of the municipality).

- Share the identified main regulatory barriers and potential alternatives with the regional and national regulatory authorities.

Identify financial and economic conditions and opportunities for circular economy initiatives

Identifying financial opportunities for circular economy initiatives would improve access to funding for circular economy projects in their start-up, implementation and scale-up phases. An option for SMEs would be, for example, to create a scheme to offer subsidised loans or credit guarantees to circular economy companies, in co-operation with private and semi-public financial institutions (e.g. banks, business funds). The idea would be for the municipality/public fund to compensate the financial institution for part of the interest rates or provide guarantees on collateral, to attach a value to the "public good" created by circular economy companies. There are several financial tools, as reported in Box 3.1.

Key actions:

- Liaise with the national government's departments to clarify existing funding opportunities and with other cities to learn about their experience.
- Create a scheme to offer subsidised loans or credit guarantees to circular economy companies, in co-operation with private and semi-public financial institutions (e.g. banks, business funds).
- Facilitate access to finance and broaden the range of financial instruments for entrepreneurship considering the available funding options and budget capabilities of the city. For example:
  - Traditional instruments: grants, soft loans, loan guarantees.
  - Alternative and non-bank sources of finance: crowdfunding, peer-to-peer lending, business angel networks, venture capital.

Box 3.1. Financing instruments for the circular economy: International practices

There are several initiatives (at the local, national and international levels) that seek to accelerate the transition to a circular economy by improving access to funding for circular economy projects:

- **Revolving funds**: The city of Amsterdam, Netherlands through the Amsterdam Climate and Energy Fund (ACEF) and the Sustainability Fund invested in more than 65 projects related to climate, sustainability and air quality for a total of EUR 30 million. The revolving funds allow to reinvest revenues within 15 years to fund additional sustainable energy production, energy efficiency or circular economy projects. Each of the funded projects must contribute to the aims of the Sustainability Agenda approved by the City Council in 2015. Regarding the nature of the financing, the ACEF provides funding in the form of loans, warranties and/or share capital, subject to a maximum of EUR 5 million per project.

- **Venture capital and growth capital**: The London Waste and Recycling Board (LWARB) supports circular businesses through the Circular Economy Business Support Programme. The venture capital fund supports circular economy small- and medium-sized enterprises (SMEs) in various steps of start-up financing and in scaling up businesses that are already in the market. Moreover, the LWARB, through the Circularity European Growth Fund 1 operated by Circularity Capital, seeks investment opportunities in circular businesses with proven cash flow and profit, which need significant capital to scale up.

- **Loans and funds**: The European Investment Bank (EIB) offers medium- and long-term loans for large scale circular economy projects and indirect financing through local banks and other agents for smaller projects, particularly related to SMEs. Other new circular economy project models can also be financed by the European Fund for Strategic Investments (EFSI),[1] and InnovFin[2]. In 2020, the EIB within the Urban Agenda Partnership for the Circular Economy launched the "Circular City Funding Guide" to provide an overview of available financing tools to cities, businesses and stakeholders wishing to advance towards a circular economy. Different types of financing tools are organised under the following categories: guarantees, equity, debt, grants and alternative funding sources.

- **Bonds**: Private banks are showing an increasing interest in the circular economy transition. In 2019, for the first time, a private Italian bank issued a "sustainable bond" for circular economy projects (EUR 750 million were allocated to this end). A Dutch bank plans to allocate EUR 1 billion in the next 5 years to finance circular projects with the objective of saving 1 million tonnes of CO2 in 5 years. Selected projects receive an initial circular assessment and are guided in the identification of circular opportunities. The network FinanCE, created in 2014, gathers commercial and public banks and institutional investors interested in supporting the circular transition.

Source: C40 Cities (2016[11]), *C40 Good Practice Guides: Amsterdam - Sustainability Fund and Amsterdam Climate and Energy Fund*, http://www.c40.org/case_studies/c40-good-practice-guides-amsterdam-sustainability-fund-and-amsterdam-climate-energy-fund (accessed on 6 June 2019); London Waste and Recycling Board (2019[12]), *London Waste and Recycling Board Website* , http://www.lwarb.gov.uk/ (accessed on 6 June 2019); EC (2019[13]), *Improving Access to Finance for Circular Economy Projects*, http://dx.doi.org/10.2777/983129; EIB (2019[14]), *The EIB Circular Economy Guide Supporting the Circular Transition*, http://www.eib.org/attachments/thematic/circular_economy_guide_en.pdf (accessed on 2 August 2019); London Waste and Recycling Board (2019[15]) *Circular Economy Investment for Businesses in London*, http://www.lwarb.gov.uk/what-we-do/circular-london/circular-economy-investment-for-businesses/ (accessed on 5 August 2019); OECD (2019[16]), *OECD Highlights of the 1st OECD Roundtable on the Circular Economy in Cities and Regions*, OECD, Paris; Urban Agenda Partnership for Circular Economy (2020[17]), *The Circular City Funding Guide*, European Investment Bank, https://www.circularcityfundingguide.eu/ (accessed on 6 February 2020); OECD (forthcoming[2]), *The Circular Economy in Cities and Regions*, Synthesis Report, OECD, Paris.

Implement Green Public Procurement

Green Public Procurement (GPP) is a strategic governance tool to foster a circular transition. Circular economy principles could be included in tenders to stimulate circular building, such as insulation and energy saving, reuse of materials, use of locally produced materials and dismantling options. The cities of Toronto (Canada), Copenhagen (Denmark), Paris (France) and Ljubljana (Slovenia) provide examples of local governments that have started to implement circular economy criteria in their public procurement procedures. The city of Ljubljana included environmental requirements in its tenders as part of the technical specifications, as a condition for determining the qualifications of the provider or as a criterion for selecting the most favourable bid. Paris was one of the first cities to adopt a scheme for responsible public procurement in February 2016. By 2018, 43% of the city's purchases were linked to the circular economy and 14% of them included "circular economy" criteria. The city of Toronto created the Circular Economy Procurement Implementation Plan and Framework to use its purchasing power as a driver for waste reduction, economic growth and social prosperity (City of Toronto, 2018[18]) In 2016, the municipality of Copenhagen defined a number of environmental criteria for public building and construction projects, such as for resource efficiency, recycling and reuse of materials (Copenhagen Municipality, 2016[19]). The municipal departments planning a building project would need to include at least two alternative materials for each building part when doing the life cycle assessment (LCA). The department will choose constructions with the lowest negative environmental impacts. At the same time, the reuse of old bricks is being promoted thorough public procurement (Salmenperä et al., 2017[20]).

Key actions:

- Include circular standards in the technical specifications, procurement selection and award criteria, as well as in contract performance clauses (e.g. reuse, durability, reparability, second-hand or remanufactured products).

- Adapt the public procurement evaluation system, highlighting the value of social and environmental ratings in comparison with the price criteria.

- Establish clear requirements in tenders in order to foster the quality, maintenance and design of products. Several tools could be applied, such as: life cycle analysis (LCA); eco-label; and eco-design.

Develop training programmes on the circular economy

The development of training programmes in the circular economy, with a sectoral focus on upstream and downstream waste management, agro-food, product re-design, and construction and demolition, in collaboration with universities and research centres, would encourage technical and non-technical capacity building among public officials, stakeholders and citizens. There are several examples of cities that promote training programmes for capacity building and sharing good practices such as the following: the Public Waste Agency of Flanders (OVAM) (Belgium) as part of "Flanders Circular" offers a Masterclass on Circular Economy. In four half-day sessions, participants discover the opportunities for their business in a circular economy. The city of Glasgow (United Kingdom) has organised workshops and events to build capacity and share good practices. The Chamber of Commerce of Glasgow also provides capacity building programmes for businesses aiming at transitioning to a circular economy.

Key actions:

- Review and analyse the required skills and capacities for carrying out all the activities associated with designing, setting, implementing and monitoring the circular economy strategy. This could include the capacity to:

- o Design circular economy plans/programmes that are realistic, result-oriented, tailored and coherent with national and regional objectives.
  - o Involve stakeholders in the planning of the circular economy strategy.
  - o Ensure adequate financial resources by linking strategic plans to multi-annual budgets and to mobilise private sector financing.
  - o Design and use monitoring indicator systems.
  - o Carry out evaluations.
- Develop targeted capacity building programmes within municipal departments (e.g. procurement, legislation).
- Develop targeted capacity building programmes for the private sector (e.g. starting with stakeholders from selected sectors).
- Start collaborations with the universities.
- Create tailored educational content on the circular economy concept for schools.

Create spaces for experimentation

Creating spaces for experimentation and sharing benefits as well as costs and risks with stakeholders would provide suitable facilities to test and pilot new circular economy projects, while encouraging collaborations. The municipality could provide experimental spaces that could also be labelled (e.g. Circular Innovation Spaces) to attract stakeholders, such as entrepreneurs and scientists. Since 2010 in Paris, France, the Urban Lab has accompanied more than 200 experiments and consolidated a methodology to support effective experimentation in 4 main stages: i) the definition of the experimental project and its evaluation; ii) a search of the experimental site; iii) the deployment of experimentation; and iv) valuation and transformation. In order to facilitate access to these experimental sites, the Urban Lab has been working for 10 years, in the development of a legal framework that start-ups can refer to for the development of their projects (e.g. a model agreement for using publicly owned spaces for a fixed period of time (Urban Lab, 2019[21]).

Key actions:

- Create spaces for experimentation, such as circular districts; streets, areas or neighbours for circular innovation and pilots; living labs and ad hoc events for co-creation;
- Set rules and objectives for the use of these spaces that can be labelled as Circular Innovation Spaces.

Develop an information, monitoring and evaluation system

Generating an information, monitoring and evaluation system would help reach a better understanding of what the circular economy is and improve policymaking and implementation. For instance, in the case of the building sector, data on material for construction would help understand what kind of materials are used for building and how they can be used in the future (see Chapter 2). Mapping empty buildings would help avoid new constructions and plan alternative use of existing ones; mapping input and output of material flows would help establish priority actions. For the future, monitoring and evaluating the achievement of set targets and goals of the circular strategy in the short, medium and long term, would represent an important feature that would help identify how "circular" the city is and what works, what does not work and what can be improved (Box 3.2).

Key actions:

- Create an information, monitoring and evaluation framework, considering environmental dimensions (e.g. resources, waste and circulation processes), material flows (water, energy, products, food, transportation, information, people) and social aspects (circular jobs created).
- Generate open data sources if possible (e.g. the publication of consistent and up-to-date information about how people and public vehicles move around the city and other forms of open data can boost the development of innovative start-ups).
- Make the most of the 5G rollout in the city by exploring its application as an enabler to circular economy-related activities, adding to the sectors already selected: health, energy, traffic, agriculture and living environment.
- Explore the innovative solutions that big data, the Internet of Things and blockchain tools can provide to the circular economy (e.g. real-time information to make last-mile logistics more efficient).
- Collect information on empty buildings, materials used for construction and waste streams and make it publicly accessible.
- Make inventories of circular economy initiatives and update them regularly.
- Make an inventory of laws and regulations that can foster the transition from a linear to a circular economy.
- Use output indicators to evaluate the results of the strategy (e.g. CO2 emissions saved, raw materials avoided, use of recovered materials, energy savings, etc.).
- Self-assess how "circular" the city is by using the OECD self-assessment framework (OECD, forthcoming[2]) (Box 3.2).
- Incorporate the information system into the online circular economy information platform that should be regularly updated and easily accessible.
- Share with citizens and stakeholders the outcomes of the strategy and the impacts through a website.

Box 3.2. The proposed OECD Circular Economy Scoreboard for Cities and Regions

The proposed OECD Circular Economy Scoreboard for cities and regions consists of a self-assessment of key governance conditions to evaluate the level of advancement towards a circular economy in cities and regions. It is composed of ten key dimensions, whose implementation governments and stakeholders can evaluate based on a scoreboard system, indicating the level of implementation of each dimension (Newcomer, In progress and Advanced).

Table 3.3. OECD Circular Economy Scoreboard for Cities and Regions

	Level of advancement		
	Newcomer	In progress	Advanced
Circular economy framework	The city/region is planning to develop a circular economy strategy but has not started yet.	The circular economy strategy is under development.	Existence of a circular economy strategy with specific goals and priorities, actions, sectors and a monitoring framework.
Co-ordination mechanisms	There are no co-ordination mechanisms in place but under development.	Existence of dialogues across levels of government, but not focused on the circular economy.	Co-ordination mechanisms across levels of governments to set and implement a circular economy

			strategy or initiative are well established and functioning.
Policy coherence	The circular economy initiatives are still not aligned with other related policy areas (e.g. climate change, sustainable development and air quality).	The circular economy initiatives are aligned with some specific related policy areas (e.g. climate change, sustainable development and air quality) but they are still fragmented.	Existence of overall policy coherence between circular economy initiatives and related policy areas (e.g. climate change, sustainable development and air quality).
Economy and finance	No current financial instruments in place but planned.	Existence of a budget dedicated to environmental spending that is foreseen to be used also for circular economy projects.	Existence of a funding programme and economic incentives for circular economy projects with specific objectives, prioritised sectors and a monitoring framework of the outcomes.
Innovation	There are no spaces to test and pilot but planned.	Design of spaces to test and pilot circular economy projects under development.	Existence of spaces to test and pilot circular economy projects.
Stakeholder engagement	Existence of an initiative for the mapping of the most relevant stakeholders in the city/region.	Existence of a dialogue with stakeholders for the design and implementation of the circular economy strategy.	Existence of participation spaces for stakeholders through which input is used for the design and implementation of circular strategies.
Capacity building	Existence of capacity building programmes on green and sustainable economy fields.	Existence of capacity building programmes for activities associated with designing, setting and implementing a circular economy initiative.	Regular capacity building programmes for activities associated with designing, setting, implementing and monitoring the circular economy strategy.
Green Public Procurement	Green Public Procurement is being developed.	Existence of a green procurement model including environmental criteria (e.g. reduction of CO2 emissions).	Existence of a circular public procurement framework (e.g. waste diversion from procurement activities, raw materials avoided and percentage of recycled content).
Data and information	Identification of data on waste management and information campaigns to prevent waste generation.	Existence of data on waste management and information campaigns on the circular economy.	Existence of an information system on the circular economy. Data are publicly available and citizens and business informed of the opportunities related to circular business models and behaviours.
Monitoring and evaluation	No monitoring or evaluation framework in place.	Existence of a monitoring and evaluation framework that includes environmental aspects.	Existence of a monitoring and evaluation framework that includes environmental, economic and social aspects.

According to the self-evaluation, the city/region will identify its own level of advancement toward the transition to a circular economy, identify gaps and set its own targets for improvement. The methodology for self-assessment consists in a scoreboard system that can indicate the level of advancement of circular cities and regions towards the transition. Sub-indicators to better specify each dimension are under development and will be tested in the case studies of the OECD Programme on the Circular Economy in Cities and Regions.

Source: OECD (forthcoming[2]), *The Circular Economy in Cities and Regions*, Synthesis Report, OECD Publishing, Paris.

References

ABC2C (2019), *Homepage*, https://abc2c.nl/over-abc2c/ (accessed on 26 July 2019). [33]

C40 Cities (2016), *C40 Good Practice Guides: Amsterdam - Sustainability Fund and Amsterdam Climate and Energy Fund*, http://www.c40.org/case_studies/c40-good-practice-guides-amsterdam-sustainability-fund-and-amsterdam-climate-energy-fund (accessed on 6 June 2019). [11]

Circle Economy/Fabric/TNO:Gemeente Amsterdam (2016), *Circular Amsterdam - A Vision and Action Agenda for the City and Metropolitan Area*, https://amsterdamsmartcity.com/projects/circle-scan-amsterdam (accessed on 30 April 2019). [36]

Circulair Friesland Association (2015), *Circulair Fryslân*, https://www.urgenda.nl/documents/CirculairFryslan2.pdf (accessed on 2 May 2019). [40]

Circular Economy Club (2019), *Renting Lighting: Schiphol Airport*, https://www.circulareconomyclub.com/solutions/renting-lighting-schiphol-airport/ (accessed on 21 February 2020). [1]

City of Amsterdam (2019), *Roadmap Circular Land Tendering*, Amsterdam Smart City, https://amsterdamsmartcity.com/projects/roadmap-circular-land-tendering (accessed on 13 February 2020). [10]

City of Paris (2015), *White Paper on the Circular Economy of Greater Paris*, https://api-site.paris.fr/images/77050 (accessed on 11 June 2019). [5]

City of Toronto (2018), *Circular Economy Procurement Implementation Plan and Framework*. [18]

CO₂ Monitor Groningen (2018), *CO₂-Monitor Groningen*, https://www.groningenco2neutraal.nl/ (accessed on 29 April 2019). [28]

Copenhagen Municipality (2016), *Environment in Construction and Civil Engineering*, https://www.kk.dk/miljoe-byggeri-anlaeg (accessed on 5 March 2020). [19]

Cradle to Cradle Products Innovation Institute (2019), *Cradle to Cradle Certified™*, http://www.c2ccertified.org/ (accessed on 30 April 2019). [34]

EC (2019), *Improving Access to Finance for Circular Economy Projects*, European Commission, http://dx.doi.org/10.2777/983129. [13]

EIB (2019), *The EIB Circular Economy Guide Supporting the Circular Transition*, European Investment Bank, http://www.eib.org/attachments/thematic/circular_economy_guide_en.pdf (accessed on 2 August 2019). [14]

Ellen MacArthur Foundation (2019), *Cities and Circular Economy for Food*, https://www.ellenmacarthurfoundation.org/assets/downloads/Cities-and-Circular-Economy-for-Food_280119.pdf (accessed on 30 April 2019). [29]

EnTranCe (2019), *About EnTranCe*, https://www.en-tran-ce.org/en/over-entrance/ (accessed on 29 April 2019). [32]

EPEA GmbH (2019), *Homepage*, https://epea-hamburg.com/ (accessed on 30 April 2019). [35]

EU Eden Project (2002), *Waste Neutral - A Sustainable Approach to Waste and Resource Management*, Eden Project, http://ec.europa.eu/environment/archives/waste/pdf_comments/eden_annex.pdf (accessed on 6 June 2019). [47]

Groningen Municipality (2019), *Chemistry*, Groningen.nl, https://groningen.nl/en/do-business/sector-information/chemistry (accessed on 29 April 2019). [44]

Groningen Municipality (2019), *Introduction to Groningen - The Circular Innovation Hub*. [25]

Groningen Municipality (2019), *Neighborhood Energy Plans*, https://gemeente.groningen.nl/wijkenergieplannen (accessed on 22 November 2019). [31]

Groningen Municipality (2019), *Proposal City of Groningen for Circular and Regenerative Cties: Focus on Industrial Areas as Regenerative Drivers for the Cities of the Future*. [42]

Groningen Municipality (2018), *Council Proposal: Groningen Circular*. [24]

Groningen Municipality (2013), *Op weg naar een groene kringloop-economie*, https://gemeente.groningen.nl/sites/default/files/groningen-visie-biobasedeconomy.pdf (accessed on 29 April 2019). [43]

House of Design (2019), *Homepage*, http://www.houseofdesign.nl/en/ (accessed on 26 July 2019). [45]

Koploperproject (2019), *Front Runner Project (Koploperproject)*, https://www.koploperproject-groningen.nl/zo-werkt-het (accessed on 26 November 2019). [26]

London Waste and Recycling Board (2019), *Circular Economy Investment for Businesses in London*, http://www.lwarb.gov.uk/what-we-do/circular-london/circular-economy-investment-for-businesses/ (accessed on 5 August 2019). [15]

London Waste and Recycling Board (2019), *London Waste and Recycling Board Website*, London Waste and Recycling Board, http://www.lwarb.gov.uk/ (accessed on 6 June 2019). [12]

Luscuere, L. (2016), "Materials passports: Optimising value recovery from materials", http://dx.doi.org/10.1680/jwarm.16.00016. [37]

LWARB (2017), *London's Circular Economy Route Map*, London Waste and Recycling Board, http://www.lwarb.gov.uk/wp-content/uploads/2015/04/LWARB-London%E2%80%99s-CE-route-map_16.6.17a_singlepages_sml.pdf (accessed on 5 August 2019). [4]

Madaster (2019), *About Us*, https://www.madaster.com/en/about-us (accessed on 30 April 2019). [38]

Metabolic (2018), "Metabolic pioneers urban and regional approaches for Circular Economy", https://www.metabolic.nl/news/metabolic-pioneers-urban-and-regional-approaches-for-circular-economy/ (accessed on 30 April 2019). [23]

Ministry of Economic Affairs (2017), *Better Regulation: Towards a Responsible Reduction in the Regulatory Burden 2012-2017*, https://www.government.nl/documents/reports/2017/08/22/better-regulation-towards-a-responsible-reduction-in-the-regulatory-burden-2012-2017 (accessed on 27 November 2019). [46]

Ministry of Infrastructure and the Environment/Ministry of Economic Affairs (2016), *A Circular Economy in the Netherlands by 2050*, https://www.government.nl/topics/circular-economy/accelerating-the-transition-to-a-circular-economy (accessed on 27 November 2019). [6]

Netherlands Enterprise Agency (2019), *Rijksdienst voor Ondernemend Nederland*, https://www.rvo.nl/ (accessed on 11 February 2020). [22]

Netherlands Entreprise Agency (2014), *Tax Relief Schemes for Environmentally Friendly Investment (Vamil and MIA)*, http://www.rvo.nl (accessed on 29 April 2019). [39]

Nord Regio (2018), *Developing and Managing Innovation Ecosystems in the Circular Economy*, http://norden.diva-portal.org/smash/get/diva2:1240777/FULLTEXT01.pdf (accessed on 6 June 2019). [48]

OECD (2019), *OECD Highlights of the 1st OECD Roundtable on the Circular Economy in Cities and Regions*, OECD, Paris. [16]

OECD (2019), *Regions in Industrial Transition: Policies for People and Places*, OECD Publishing, Paris, https://dx.doi.org/10.1787/c76ec2a1-en. [8]

OECD (2016), *Water Governance in Cities*, https://www.oecd-ilibrary.org/governance/water-governance-in-cities_9789264251090-en (accessed on 6 February 2020). [27]

OECD (2015), *Stakeholder Engagement for Inclusive Water Governance*, OECD Studies on Water, OECD Publishing, Paris, https://dx.doi.org/10.1787/9789264231122-en. [3]

OECD (2013), *Rural-Urban Partnerships: An Integrated Approach to Economic Development*, OECD Rural Policy Reviews, OECD Publishing, Paris, https://dx.doi.org/10.1787/9789264204812-en. [9]

OECD (2010), *The One Stop Shop Concept: Best Practices for Benchmarking Training Workshop on One Stop Shop Services for Investors in the MENA Region*, OECD, Paris. [7]

OECD (forthcoming), *The Circular Economy in Cities and Regions*, Synthesis Report, OECD, Paris. [2]

Reuters (2019), "Netherlands to halt Groningen gas production by 2022 - Reuters", https://www.reuters.com/article/us-netherlands-gas/netherlands-to-halt-groningen-gas-production-by-2022-idUSKCN1VV1KE (accessed on 26 November 2019). [30]

Salmenperä, H. et al. (2017), *Circular Public Procurement in the Nordic Countries*, TemaNord, Nordic Council of Ministers, Copenhagen, https://dx.doi.org/10.6027/TN2017-512. [20]

Urban Agenda Partnership for Circular Economy (2020), *The Circular City Funding Guide*, European Investment Bank, https://www.circularcityfundingguide.eu/ (accessed on 6 February 2020). [17]

Urban Lab (2019), *Pourquoi l'Urban Lab ?*, https://urbanlab.parisandco.paris/Notre-offre/Pourquoi-l-Urban-Lab (accessed on 13 February 2020). [21]

Van Wijnen (2019), *Circulariteit*, https://www.vanwijnen.nl/thema/circulariteit-2/ (accessed on 5 June 2019). [41]

Notes

[1] For more information: www.eib.org/en/efsi/index.htm.

[2] For more information: www.eib.org/en/products/blending/innovfin/.

Annex A. List of stakeholders consulted during the policy dialogue

Institution	Name
ABC2	Maarten Wiersma
Attero	Marco Kwak
Avebe	Johan Russchen
Bio Clean Earth	Sytze Keuning
City of Groningen	Aline Otten
City of Groningen	Anne Helbig
City of Groningen	Floor de Jong
City of Groningen	Gerard Verelst
City of Groningen	Hendrik Jan Withag
City of Groningen	Miriam Hall
DAAD	Sjoerd Tasseron
DaaromWel – Social entrepreneur	Mathijs Niehaus
Enexis	Fokko Reinders
EPS Netherlands	Henk Bos
Groningen Seaports	Henri Kats
Hanze University of Applied Sciences	Klaas Jan Noorman
House of Design	Eileen Blackmore
Kaaskop	Cor Dijkstra
KNN Advies	Cor Kamminga
Laifennuver	Pier Tjepkema
Marketing Groningen	Barbara Risselada
Marketing Groningen	Rik Ruiter
New Energy Coalition	Martijn de Vries
NOM (Northern Development Company/Society)	Rudmer Heij
Northern Innovation Lab Circular Economy (NICE)	Alex van Oost
Province of Friesland	Deborah Ligthart
Province of Friesland	Sander Bos
Province of Friesland	Tjeerd Hazenberg
Province of Groningen	Pieter Jan Boumeister
Region Groningen Assen	Guus Receveur
Royal Haskoning DHV	Michael Freerks
Royal Haskoning DHV	Sebastiaan van der Haar
Schilders de Vries	Roelof de Vries
Stainkoeln	Gelmer Haveman
Suikerunie	Teun van der Weg

Institution	Name
Toentje	Jos Meijers
Triade	Edward van der Meer
Triade	Ronald Hesse
Triade	Sven Stielstra
TSI Foundation	Peter Everts
van Afval	Henk Alssema
van Wijnen	Elze Reitsema
Waterschap Noorderzijlvest – Water Authority	Tjitse Mollema

Printed by Libri Plureos GmbH in Hamburg,
Germany